'A man of immense learning, he was interested in this borderline zone [*Mitteleuropa*], with its fusion of Latin and Slavic cultures, presumably because he sensed in their interplay the future of European civilization.' – Joseph Brodsky

'Imagine an impossible combination of Flann O'Brien and Isaiah Berlin. Well, Butler comes close.' – Ferdinand Mount

'An odyssey, from Ireland to East, West and back again: stemming from and returning to an intellecutal tradition which takes in Montaigne and Turgenev as well as Swift and Shaw . . . It moves like a searchlight, to take in and illuminate the largest questions imaginable.' – R. F. Foster

'To follow Hubert Butler is to enjoy the hair-raising frisson of history passing by.' – Eoghan Harris

Hubert Butler was born in Kilkenny in 1900 and educated in England at Charterhouse and St John's College, Oxford. After work with the Irish County Libraries in the mid-1920s he travelled extensively throughout Europe, before returning in 1941 to Co. Kilkenny, where he lived – as market gardener, broadcaster, journalist and historian – until his death in 1991. He won international recognition during his lifetime with the publication of three volumes of essays, *Escape from the Anthill* (1985), *The Children of Drancy* (1988) and *Grandmother and Wolfe Tone* (1990).

John Banville's novels include *The Book of Evidence*, *The Sea* and The Infinities. He reviews frequently for the *Irish Times*, the *Guardian* and the *New York Review of Books*.

Hubert Butler

—

THE INVADER WORE SLIPPERS

—

European Essays

Edited by John Banville

Notting Hill Editions

Published in 2012
by Notting Hill Editions Ltd
Newcombe House, 45 Notting Hill Gate
London W11 3LQ

Designed by FLOK Design, Berlin, Germany
Typeset by CB editions, London

Printed and bound
by Memminger MedienCentrum, Memmingen, Germany

Copyright © The Estate of Hubert Butler and The Lilliput Press, 1985, 1988, 1990, 1996
Introduction and this selection copyright © 2012 by John Banville

All rights reserved

The right of John Banville to be identified as the editor of this work has been asserted in accordance with Section 77 of the Copyright, Designs and Patents Act 1998

This book is sold subject to the condition that it shall not, by way of trade or otherwise, be lent, resold, hired out or otherwise circulated without the publisher's prior consent in any form of binding or cover other than that in which it is published and without a similar condition including this condition being imposed on the subsequent purchaser

A CIP record for this book
is available from the British Library

ISBN 978-1-907-90351-9

www.nottinghilleditions.com

Contents

- Introduction by John Banville -
vii

- Sources & Acknowledgements -
xvii

- 'The City' by C. P. Cavafy -
(trans. Hubert Butler)
2

- Riga Strand in 1930 (1930) -
3

- Report on Yugoslavia (1947) -
18

- The Last Izmerenje (1947) -
39

- The Invader Wore Slippers (1950) -
54

- In Russia (1956/57) -
71

- Mr Pfeffer of Sarajevo (1956) -
88

- The Final Solution (1962) -
107

- Carl von Ossietzky (1964) -
131

- A Visit to Hesse and Some Thoughts about Princes (1968) -
137

- The Children of Drancy (1968/78) -
145

- Peter's Window (1984) -
163

- The Artukovitch File (1985) -
217

- The Kagran Gruppe (1988) -
255

John Banville

– Introduction –

It is surely a nice irony that although Hubert Butler throughout his life repeatedly asserted the importance of local history over a pretentious concern with national or international affairs, he was one of the most travelled Irishmen of his time. That time was the greater part of the twentieth century – he was born in 1900 and died in 1991 – and he spent much of it abroad, living or travelling in Russia, the Balkans, China, America. He had a deep curiosity about and interest in the modes of living adopted by peoples strange to him, yet one of the abiding themes in all his writings is the fatuousness of our modern-day concern for the universal at the expense of the particular. He wrote that when his essays 'appear to be about Russia or Greece or Spain or Yugoslavia, they are really about Ireland,'[1] a focus that, he declared, for him had never varied.

Butler was born at Maidenhall, the family's ancestral home, a modest Georgian mansion near Bennettsbridge in County Kilkenny. His ancestors had been among the first English settlers in Ireland after the annexation of the country in the twelfth century by King

1.'Introduction to *Escape from the Anthill* (1985), p.2.

Henry II. The Butlers flourished and multiplied, and in time became the Dukes of Ormonde, owners of vast estates and builders of much of Georgian Dublin. Hubert Butler was quietly proud of his family, and founded the Butler Society and edited the society's journal until his death. The first essay printed here, 'A Visit to Hesse and Some Thoughts About Princes', is a subtle declaration of the importance of what would now be called the extended family, and a reaffirmation of the Butlerian principle of 'near is far,' as well as a mild defence of the role within culture of a natural aristocracy. The piece is an account of a Butler Society outing to Germany to visit the 'several castles and mansions of the von Buttlars of Hesse, who claim kinship with the Irish and English Butlers.'[2] The rulers of the old German princedoms, he writes,

> were, of course, very ordinary people, operating in a familiar social cycle. Were the petty princes of Italy during the Renaissance very different? Robbers became robber barons, who became barons, who became the victims of robbers, who became . . . Irish history makes the process well known to us.[3]

Butler was educated in England, at Charterhouse and Oxford, after which he returned home and worked in the Irish County Library Service, and was, as he wrote, a 'disciple' of Sir Horace Plunkett,

2. See below, p.137.
3. Ibid., p.143.

— *Introduction* —

the initiator of the Irish Co-operative movement. Later, in the Thirties, he traveled widely in Europe, and worked as a teacher of English in Egypt and Russia. In the mid-1930s he spent three years in Yugoslavia on a scholarship from the London School of Slavonic Studies. In 1941, on the death of his father, he came back and settled at Maidenhall, 'to live in the place where I was born and where my father, grandfather and great-grandfather had lived before me.'[4]

Thus was set the pattern of the rest of his life. Yet he was anything but parochial in his outlook and interests, and he continued to travel, to observe and to write on a wide variety of subjects, from family history to Celtic hagiography to world politics. This champion of the local was of a decidedly pluralist cast of mind. In 'The Barriers',[5] a splendid piece published in the Irish magazine *The Bell* in 1941, during some of the darkest days of the war, he reminded neutral Ireland that 'self-sufficiency is in fact insufficient for a national culture.'

Great cultures have always risen from the interaction of diverse societies. And where that interaction has been varied, easy and reciprocated, as between the city-states of Greece, or during the Renaissance, national genius has expressed itself most freely.

---

4. Introduction to *Escape from the Anthill* (1985), p.2.
5. This essay can be found in the companion volume of Butler's essays, *The Eggman and the Fairies*, also published by Notting Hill Editions (2012).

— THE INVADER WORE SLIPPERS —

One of Butler's early formative experiences was the winter that he spent in Leningrad – formerly, and now again, St Petersburg – teaching English at a state institute. The long essay 'Peter's Window' is a frank, racy, and wonderfully evocative account of this adventure, when Soviet Communism was at its most violently paranoid. 'In the end,' Butler writes, 'I came to the conclusion that almost all those whom I was able to see constantly had obtained the consent of the GPU and were under obligation to report my movements.'[6] Here, as so often, Butler refuses to strike a dramatic or self-dramatising tone. In his understated fashion, however, he catches the mood of the time and place with a novelist's eye – and nose: 'Over the whole flat there was that sweetish, musty smell of black bread and benzine and scent and galoshes that Russians seem to carry with them, even into exile. I felt lonely and ill at ease.'[7]

A large part of that unease was the sense he and so many others had at the time of the inevitability and imminence of another world war. On this subject, too, Butler maintains a deceptive mildness of tone. In one of his finest essays, 'The Invader Wore Slippers,' written in 1950, he recalls how, during the war, 'we in Ireland heard much of the jackboot and how we should be trampled beneath it if Britain's protection failed us,' and how 'our imagination, fed on the daily press, showed us a Technicolor picture of barbarity and heroism.'

6. See below, p.179.
7. Ibid., p.168.

— *Introduction* —

We did not ask ourselves: 'Supposing the invader wears not jackboots, but carpet slippers, or patent-leather pumps, how will I behave, and the respectable X's, the patriotic Y's and the pious Z's?' How could we? The newspapers told us only about the jackboots.[8]

He then goes on to examine the reaction of the native populations of the Channel Islands, of Brittany and Croatia, when the delicately shod Nazi invaders came strolling in. He is particularly scathing about the way in which the Channel Islanders accepted German occupation and settled back into their comfortable lives as before.

The readers of the *Guernsey Evening Post* were shocked and repelled no doubt to see articles by Goebbels and Lord Haw-Haw, but not to the pitch of stopping their subscriptions. How else could they advertise their cocker spaniels and their lawn mowers or learn about the cricket results?[9]

Although he does not say so directly, it is obvious that Butler harboured very grave doubts about how Ireland, for instance, would have behaved if there had been an invasion. In 'The Kagran Gruppe', an account of Butler's work among Austrian Jews in the terrible year 1938–9, he quotes a telling declaration made in the Irish parliament in 1943 by Oliver J. Flanagan, who as a member of Fine Gael, the second-largest

8. Ibid., p.54.
9. Ibid., p.59.

party in the country, was to be a self-appointed guardian of Irish faith and morals into the 1980s: ' "There is one thing," he said, "that the Germans did and that was to rout the Jews out of their country." He added that we should rout them out of Ireland: "They crucified our Saviour 1,900 years ago and they have been crucifying us every day of the week." No one contradicted him.'[10]

In the essay 'The Artukovitch File', Butler follows the postwar trail of the Minister of the Interior in Ante Pavelitch's uniquely brutal regime in Croatia under the Nazis. 'Pavelitch's terrible campaign of compulsory conversion of Orthodox Christians,' he writes, 'resulted in some of the worst religious massacres that have ever happened in European history.'[11] – this was written, of course, decades before the Serbian campaign of 'ethnic cleansing' and the extermination of Bosnian Muslims in the 1990s. When Pavelitch fell, Andrija Artukovitch escaped via Austria and Switzerland, eventually settling in California. On the way to America he had lived for a year in Ireland under an alias. US visas for him and his family were procured through the Irish government, who provided him with false papers. Butler's outrage at this enormity on the part of his own countrymen is expressed with his usual understated elegance – 'The process by which a great persecutor is turned into a martyr is surely an interesting one that

10. Ibid, p.256.
11. Ibid., p.27.

— *Introduction* —

needs the closest investigation'[12] — but we are left in no doubt about his contempt for the 'patriotic Y's and the pious Z's' who would connive at the escape from justice of a man who had taken an active part in some of the most atrocious deeds of the war.

Butler acknowledges the centrality to our time of the Nazi death camps — Auschwitz, he declares, is the greatest single crime in human history — but he is determined that even such heinousness will not overshadow the many other atrocities this century has witnessed. He was one of the first in the West to draw attention to the campaign of forced conversion to Roman Catholicism of 2.5 million Orthodox Serbs under the reign of Pavelitch. The campaign resulted in the slaughter of untold tens of thousands of Orthodox Serbs. He quotes from a memorandum from exiled Serbs to the United Nations in 1950:

It is stated that a Franciscan had been commandant of Jasenovac, the worst and biggest of the concentration camps for Serbs and Jews (he had personally taken part in murdering the prisoners . . .). The memorandum relates how the focal centre for the forced conversions and the massacres had been the Franciscan monastery of Shiroki Brieg in Herzegovina (Artukovitch had been educated there), and how in 1942 a young man who was a law student at the college and a member of the Crusaders, a catholic organization, had won a prize in a competition for the slaughter of the Orthodox by cutting the

12. Ibid., p.237.

throats of 1,360 Serbs with a special knife. The prize had been a gold watch, a silver service, a roast suckling pig and some wine.[13]

When, after the war, Butler sought to bring these appalling crimes to public attention, he found himself ostracised in his own country. The Catholic Church had refused to acknowledge that the conversions of the Orthodox Serbs had been forced or had involved violence. At a public meeting in Dublin, Butler attempted to read a paper on the issue, but after a few sentences the Papal Nuncio walked out, whereupon the meeting was halted. Next morning the Irish edition of the *Sunday Express* carried the headline: "Pope's Envoy Walks Out. Government to Discuss Insult to Nuncio."

All the local government bodies of the city and county held special meetings to condemn the 'Insult'. There were speeches from mayors, ex-mayors, aldermen, creamery managers. The county council expelled me from one of its subcommittees, and I was obliged to resign from another committee. Although my friends put up a fight, I was forced to give up the honorary secretaryship of the Kilkenny Archaeological Society, which I had myself revived and guided through seven difficult years.

In effect, he was forced into internal exile. It was, in that place, in those times, a familiar story.

Like many liberals, Butler displays an unrelenting hostility towards science and its depredations – al-

13. Ibid., p.227.

— *Introduction* —

though what he calls 'science' is in reality applied science, that is, technology. 'The Children of Drancy,' a heartbreaking essay on the deportation of 4,051 Jewish children to Auschwitz in 1942, through the transit camp at Drancy near Paris – part of an operation recalled recently in a fine commemorative speech of atonement by the French President François Hollande – opens out into a superb, angry meditation on public indifference to the fate of the Jews during the war, in which Butler excoriates the champions of scientific progress, such as the novelist C.P. Snow, who in the 1960s drew attention to the widening chasm between the 'Two Cultures' of science and the humanities.

Yet castigation is not Butler's true mode. Again and again his natural curiosity leads him to examine the particulars in even the most momentous examples of human folly and mischief. In 'Peter's Window' he recalls that in 1931, while much of the Soviet Union was being laid waste by Stalinist policies and famine was about to engulf the countryside, the things he and his friends talked about in Leningrad were 'spoons, buttons, macaroni, galoshes, macaroni again. I don't believe I ever heard anyone mention Magnetogorsk or the liquidation of the kulaks of any of the remote and monstrous contemporary happenings to which by a complicated chain of causes our lifestyle and our macaroni were linked.[14]

14. Ibid., p.191.

It is for this honesty, as well as for his dry irony and muted humour, that we value Hubert Butler and his writings. He understood, better than most, the limitations of the individual as well as the individual's power if not to change things then at least to meliorate them. He refuses to present himself as a shrewd observer at the centre of great events – very few of us, he knows, get to hold Thermopylae at the head of a few hundred men or ride on a tank into liberated Paris – yet he never discounts the importance of true and necessary witness. At the close of 'Peter's Window' he presents, with typical lightness, and humility, his creed as a writer and a man: 'I am more inclined to apologise for writing about great events, which touched me not at all, than for tracing again the tiny snail track which I made myself.'[15]

---

15. Ibid., p.216.

– Sources & Acknowledgements –

The present selection of Hubert Butler's European essays is the companion to an earlier selection (*The Eggman and the Fairies: Irish Essays*, Notting Hill Editions, 2012). The essays are dated and ordered in chronological order of composition.

Sources and acknowledgements for *The Eggman and the Fairies: Irish Essays* and *The Invader Wore Slippers: European Essays*:

'The Barriers': *The Bell*, July 1941.
'New Geneva in Waterford': *Journal of the Royal Society of Antiquaries of Ireland*, December 1947.
'Boycott Village': *The Twentieth Century*, January 1958.
'The Eggman and the Fairies': *The Twentieth Century*, July 1960.
'Wolfe Tone and the Common Name of Irishman': Talk given in the Mansion House, Dublin, 24 September 1963 – the bicentenary of Wolfe Tone's birth; published as Lilliput Pamphlets/5 in 1985.
'*The Bell*: An Anglo-Irish View': *Irish University Review*, Spring 1976.
'Topical Thoughts on Shaw': *The Irish Times*, 8 January 1976, subsequently revised.
'Three Friends': *The Irish Times*, 21 February 1970.

'Beside the Nore': *Ireland of the Welcomes*, May–June 1970 (as 'Nore and Barrow').

'The City': *The Irish Times*, 10 April 1948.

'Report on Yugoslavia': Typescript of report to the War Resisters International Conference, Shrewsbury, England, August 1947.

'The Last Izmerenje': *The Irish Press*, 28 February 1947.

'The Invader Wore Slippers': *The Bell*, November 1940.

'In Russia': Sections I and II, *The Irish Times*, 6 November 1956 and 7-8 January 1957.

'Mr Pfeffer of Sarajevo': *Nonplus* (Dublin), Winter 1960.

'The Final Solution': *The Irish Times*, 3–6 June 1963.

'Carl von Ossietzky': *The Irish Times*, 6 June 1954.

'A Visit to Hesse and Some Thoughts about Princes': *The Irish Times*, 20 September 1968, and *Journal of the Butler Society* 1978/9.

'The Children of Drancy': *The Irish Review*, No. 4, Spring 1988.

'Peter's Window': (ed.) Robert Greacen, *Irish Harvest* (New Frontiers Press 1946), under the title 'The Teaching Brigade'; subsequently revised and expanded.

'The Artukovitch File': Section I appeared in *New Blackfriars*, February 1971, under the title 'What Became of Arkutovitch? Reflections on a Croatian Crusade'.

The essays in both the present selection and its companion, *The Eggman and the Fairies*, were originally collected in the following volumes, all published by The Lilliput Press, Dublin: *Escape from the Anthill* (1985), *The Children of Drancy* (1988), *Grandmother and Wolfe Tone* (1990), *In the Land of Nod* (1996).

– THE INVADER WORE SLIPPERS –

– 'The City' by C. P. Cavafy –
[1948]

You said: 'I'll seek some other land, with sails unfurled.
I'll find a worthier town than this and some serener clime.
For here ambition foiled is like a crime,
the quickening impulse of the heart is dead,
and sluggish thoughts entomb the past like lead.
Whichever way eyes glance or footsteps go,
the embers of a burnt-out ardour glow,
the scorched and broken years into the ash-pit hurled.'

You'll find no other lands, my friend, speeding with sails unfurled.
Your city will go with you. Through its streets and squares
you'll still be strolling, as you strolled, despite your prayers.
You'll age beside the hearth you once held dear,
thinking familiar thoughts. No ship will steer
your heart, new-fallowed, to a virgin strand.
You wrecked your life in this poor, stubborn land.
It's wrecked beyond repair for all the world.

(*Translated by Hubert Butler from the Greek of C. P. Cavafy, in memory of James Joyce and Trieste*)

– Riga Strand in 1930 –
[1930]

Once a week in the summer months, a pleasure steamer berths in Reval harbour and for a few hours troops of excited English tourists swoop down on the town, swarm up the hill, and penetrate in charabancs as far as Pirita and St Brigid's abbey. It is a charming spot; the views, the churches, the crooked narrow streets, compact, accessible and picturesque, are just what is required. Though they straggle off unshepherded in fifty different directions, they meet each other in a few minutes with glad cries in antique shops and cathedrals where everybody speaks English. When the hooter calls them back to the ship they have seen everything and yet are not exhausted.

The same ship wisely seldom stops at Riga. Riga is big and sprawling and new looking; it has clean, cosmopolitan boulevards, public parks, and large exhausting museums; the few tourists have a harried look and the hours pass in catching trams, changing money and haggling with droshky drivers. There are, it is true, a great many English people in Riga, but they are a serious, residential tribe, the complete reverse of the sightseers of Reval or Helsingfors. The Riga Britons are homesick and resentful businessmen who have come to buy timber and find that the Letts don't want to sell it, or bored and studious soldiers who have come to learn Russian and find that the Letts don't want to teach it. Their subsequent stories of Riga and Latvia are naturally coloured by their experiences. The timber merchants are confronted with the petty officialdom of a young nation, proud of its new independence and snatching at all opportunities of asserting it. The officers are met with blank surprise; their shy, stumbling sentences get no encouraging response from the Letts, for Russian is out of favour and they find their society restricted to the English Club and a few embittered Russian aristocrats to whom Latvia is only a rebellious province, governed by the lower orders. No wonder then that officers and merchants have no rosy memories of Riga; grudgingly perhaps they repeat the legend that the Riga air is very good and that Schwarz's is the best cafe between Berlin and Tokyo, though they've never been to Tokyo and Schwarz's is very much like other cafes; they bring home amber necklaces and caviare and polished birchwood cigarette cases, but they don't conceal that they are thankful to be out of Riga and would gladly never return.

All the same Riga Strand must have a fascination for more leisured visitors, who have time to be interested in the past and the future of the small republics which rose from the ruins of the Russian Empire. It is the holiday ground not only for Letts but for all the newly liberated peoples of the Baltic. There one may meet

— Riga Strand in 1930 —

Estonians and Finns, Lithuanians and Poles, bathing side by side with Germans, Russians and Swedes, who were once their masters.

Of all the Baltic nations perhaps the Letts have suffered the most, yet their story is typical. Their nationality and their language have survived a double conquest and many centuries of foreign rule. From the west came the Teutonic knights bearing with them a German culture and occupying the ancient territories of Lett and Lithuanian and Estonian, as far as the Finnish marshes and the empire of the Tsars. Russia too was expanding. Peter the Great was casting covetous eyes upon the Baltic and at last the 'Baltic Barons' in their turn, and all their possessions, passed under the Russian eagles. The Letts now found that they had not one master but two, for the Russians respected the Barons for their solidity and thrift and good husbandry, and confirmed them in their possessions, giving them in return for their loyalty high places at court and in the army. Ever since Peter the Great had first turned the eye of Russia westward, German culture and methods had been admired and imitated. Catherine the Great was a German, and she and her successors often chose advisers from their German subjects. The Baltic Barons found that they lost nothing by their incorporation in the Russian Empire.

If the Barons were the most privileged of the Tsar's subjects, the Letts whom they oppressed were the most wretched ... their very existence was denied, the name of Latvia was abandoned, and the Baltic lands divided into Russian provinces in which the racial differences were carefully ignored. The Letts had no appeal from the caprice of their masters; an early law limited flogging to thirty-six strokes, but humane legislation did not go much further and the Letts remained all but serfs till late on in the last century. Lettish schools were closed and Lettish newspapers prohibited, even old songs and customs that might remind them of their national past were suppressed. Every year in the old days there had been a great festival of song, the rallying point of national feeling, and every town and village had its band of singers. But the rulers recognized that a song can be more dangerous than a sword and the festival was rigorously suppressed.

Many Letts joined revolutionary organizations and, when the Revolution of 1905 broke out, the great rehearsal for the Revolution of 1917, there was an abortive revolt in Riga. A Lettish Republic was declared and for a few days maintained. The Tsar was alarmed, concessions were promised, and, when all danger was averted, forgotten: the Barons, momentarily panic-stricken, recovered their composure. But the Letts persevered, their time had not yet come, and the Great War found them still trusting in the clemency of the Tsar. It was an occasion when all the subject races must be rallied to the Russian cause, and the Baltic peoples, who were disaffected and lived upon the frontiers of

— *Riga Strand in 1930* —

the enemy, must at all costs be conciliated. The German emperor had promised to establish a Lettish Republic, and the Barons, who took this with a grain of salt, were many of them ready to welcome a German invasion. The moment was propitious for a generous gesture from Nicolas II. He agreed to grant a request hitherto persistently refused; henceforward the Letts might serve under their own officers as a separate Lettish unit. Lettish regiments were formed and graciously permitted to defend their fatherland and promised that when they had beaten the enemy they would enjoy equal rights with the Barons. There were rejoicings in Riga, and the credulous Letts believed that at last the day of their deliverance was at hand; but those who were more discerning guessed that whoever won, the Letts would be the losers, the Barons would not be shifted and the emperors would find good reasons for forgetting their solemn pledges. But as often occurs the most discerning were wrong. The unexpected, the impossible happened: both sides were defeated, Kaiser Wilhelm lost his throne and the line of Peter the Great came to a tragic end at Ekaterinburg. Yet at first it seemed as if Latvia would merely be smothered in the collapse of the two empires. By the Treaty of Brest-Litovsk Russia treacherously abandoned Latvia to Germany and after the Armistice the Allies allowed the Germans to remain in Riga to keep the country safe from Bolsheviks.

Then followed eighteen months of terrible suffering for Latvia. The Letts drove out the Bolsheviks in the east only to find the Germans in their rear, and a third enemy appeared suddenly, for an army of White Russian exiles, mobilized in Berlin, tried to conquer Latvia as a base for an attack on Russia. White and Red and Balt and German alternately ravaged the land, for their landlord barons made common cause against the Letts. But the Letts fought like tigers. At last, after foreign intervention and unheard of struggles, peace was restored, boundaries were traced by English colonels and professors, and the Latvian Republic was proclaimed.

Now at last the Letts are masters of Riga Strand, and on a June morning the sands are alive with holiday-makers. Where do they all come from? Outside Riga the pinewoods and the wastelands stretch empty and interminable, dotted here and there only with a few ramshackle wooden huts, and Riga itself does not suggest an unlimited supply of pleasure-seekers. Granted that some of them come from abroad the answer is that a seaside holiday is not so much a luxury in Latvia as a necessity. There is scarely a clerk or artisan in Riga too humble to have a rickety wooden dacha for his family during the summer months, and from there he commutes daily.

A great broad shore fringed with pinewoods sweeps round the gulf of Riga as far as eye can see: the sea is almost tideless and yet the beach is always deep and soft and clean, for the wind blows away the bus tickets and the paper bags and buries orange peel and match boxes deep in the sand. Then during the long winters the snow and the frost scavenge round the shuttered dachas, there are mountains of ice and the whole Gulf is frozen over, so that a year or two ago two men skated forty miles across the sea to the small island of Runo, but when they got there they did not recognize it for it too was covered with ice.

June when it comes finds the scene completely changed: the syringas are in blossom, the railway is opened and the post office and the post mistress are established; there are bands and cinemas and charabancs, and people run about the shady streets in dressing-gowns. Riga Strand is awake again. It is an annual metamorphosis, a conspiracy between man and nature that has started afresh every season since the first dacha went up in the pinewoods. There is a story that it belonged to a Scottish merchant and that he called it Edinburga thus giving its name to one of the seven villages of Riga Strand. Another of the villages is called Dubbelin though the Irish merchant who founded it is only a legend. In any case the villages bear little resemblance to their namesakes. Behind them, parallel to the shore, flows the broad river Aar; in front of them stretches the coastline. There is nothing to interrupt the long monotonous shore; one may walk and walk and still the landmarks keep the same place upon the horizon. There are no rock-pools nor seaweeds nor shells nor birds; sea and land meet each other with a minimum of detail and complication. One might walk to Lithuania and meet scarcely anything but water and sand and trees and sky.

There are three sandbanks that stretch round the whole of the Latvian coast as if to grade the depths for bathers; children can splash about in front of the first, while their parents sleep contentedly on the shore, but only the most intrepid swimmers venture beyond the third. In general, though, the Letts are very well used to the sea and the attendants have placed the long line of basket chairs with their backs to the waves, so that the occupants can watch the stream of people passing by under the restaurants in striped Turkish dressing-gowns and bathing-dresses far too modish to bathe in. The serious bathers do not wear bathing-dresses at all, for the beach belongs to the men till eight o'clock in the morning, when they must give place to the women, who have it to themselves till midday.

The villages themselves are scattered among the trees, long grassy tracks run parallel to each other, criss-crossed by others and fringed with wooden dachas. Here and there is an outcrop of cinemas and dance-halls. There are more pretentious buildings too with archways and gardens; they are empty and dilapidated but not with age for carved in the stone doorways one can often read 1905 or 1908 or 1912. Those were the great days of Riga strand when wealthy merchants from Moscow and St Petersburg or noblemen who did not despise Russian resorts came here with their fami-

— *Riga Strand in 1930* —

lies. Mineral springs and mud-baths were discovered and exploited; though Riga Strand was not beautiful like Finland yet it was close at hand and it was not as expensive or as exclusive as the Crimea; at least it only excluded the Jews and they were excluded as a matter of course from every chic imperial resort. There was an imperial decree forbidding them to Riga Strand.

For a decade or more all went well; new wings were constructed, new gardens laid out, fashionable specialists built up practices, more and more medicinal baths were opened – then all at once the same fate overtook the villages of Riga Strand that extinguished all the pleasure resorts of Western Europe. But the Great War, which cast only a passing blight upon the others, eclipsed for ever the brief splendours of the Latvian shore. The Baltic lands fell out of favour with the Russians, their 'barons' were suspected of intriguing with the enemy; for years it was discovered they had been employing German spies as their foresters and now from being courted they were shunned.

Then began the long campaign among the swamps and forests of Northern Europe . . . slowly the Russians fell back and their armies melted away; Bolshevik and German and White Russian swept over land and devastated it. In Riga telegraph wires were pulled down; rope had run short but there were still men to hang.

Riga Strand has emerged from the terror now and there are visitors there once more, but the clients for whom the casinos and the dance-halls and the rickety palaces of 1910 were built are gone for ever. Where now are her wealthy St Petersburg patrons, where is St Petersburg itself? Even if they wished to come, there are barbed wire entaglements six foot high, manned by armed sentries, that can only be crossed with a stack of passports. The Japanese garden with its little bridges and artificial jungles is knee-deep in groundsel and toadstools; there are trenches still and tangles of rusty barbed wire round the sulphur springs at Kemmeri, and the fashionable specialists have no prodigal Caucasian Princes to diet in their sanatoria, they have to haggle with Jewesses about mud-baths and superfluous fat. The disinherited have come into their own, the Jews have descended like locusts on Riga Strand . . . for them it has the fascination of a forbidden land. Synagogues begin to oust the gleaming onion towers and Assari, the farthest of the resorts, has almost become a Jewish village. Jewish ladies emerge with blonde curls from the hairdressers, for there are two or three 'frisetavas' in every street and Lettish gentlemen prefer blondes. But the Jews have still to mind their step, for the Letts have inherited many of the prejudices of their masters; they too fear and despise the Jews, just as they themselves were despised by the Russians.

In the afternoon the sun beats down scorchingly on Riga Strand, the pinetrees are too far away to lend their shade and even beneath them the sand is parched and burning. There are a few boatmen, a few bathers, some

— *Riga Strand in 1930* —

ladies stretched in deck chairs under the shady walls of a sanatorium, and in the long coarse grass between the pinewoods and the sand the day-trippers lie like logs. It is so quiet that one can hear a baby crying in the next village, the hoot of a steamer on the Aar, a man knocking the sand out of his shoe upon an upturned boat. It is nearly five o'clock and soon the bells begin to ring for tea in all the pensions and lodging-houses along the beach. The sanatorium bell clangs like a fire-engine, the ladies in the deckchairs clap their hands to their ears and scream at the matron, but she has been preparing the tea while they were sleeping and swings it all the harder.

After tea the beach becomes awake again, the dacha residents come out with watering-cans and make puddles in the grey powder of their flower-beds. The earth has forgotten how to drink and for a moment the water sits in a curved bubble on the surface or forms little pellets with the sand. In any case a garden in Latvia is an unnatural thing . . . the flowers in the dachas are tenants for the season like their owners. None of them looks permanent or settled; geraniums and petunias flush up a dizzy scarlet or purple for a month or two like a local inflammation, and die down the moment the owner and his watering-can have departed. The big restaurants do not even bother about bedding plants but on a gala night, the night for instance, of the firemen's ball, a cart arrives from the country piled high with branches and in half an hour the cafe is embedded in a luxuriant forest and flowers and shrubs have sprung up out of the dry sand. There are no gardens in the country either; sometimes someone will stick a peony or a dahlia into the grass, but if it does not look after itself, no one else will – and its life is usually a prolonged battle.

As the night falls more people stream out onto the strand, for the air is cool and the sinking sun has spilt a pink light across the shore. It is the hour for the evening stroll, and from dacha and sanatorium the same familiar figures emerge. There are three robust Finnish ladies, the wives of foresters, a German financier and a Lithuanian governess. There is an Estonian gentleman who is very popular with many different ladies in turn; he has friendly charming manners and is always beautifully dressed and carries a cane. He varies the ladies not because he is fickle but because sooner or later they each of them discover that he is stupid almost to mental deficiency. There is a Swedish lady who has come over to cure her pale small son from vomiting. She has a jealous husband who condemns her yearly to dull provincial watering places and Riga, she thinks, is the dullest of them all. She has a new dress for every meal but her evening parties with kisses for forfeits are not well attended. She started to have English lessons from a British officer and amid shrieks of merry badinage learnt 'I luv you so' and 'keess-meequeek' and then she got bored again. All the upper classes are bored on Riga Strand. 'Ochen skoochno!'

— *Riga Strand in 1930* —

'Sehr langweilig!' 'I'm bored stiff!' It is only good form to be bored.

A more independent type is the Russian lady who lives with her widowed mother in a dacha up the strand. She is severe, uncompromising. Every morning she does Catherine wheels, nude, on the beach for the good of her figure and in the afternoons she mortifies herself by giving Russian lessons to French and English officers. It is a degrading occupation for an aristocrat, and she slaps down her instructions with callous, disdainful efficiency. They want to study Bolshevik idioms and the new alphabet and she has forced herself to master even that. In the back room she stows away her lonely garrulous old mother and the Lettish husband, whom she married to get out of Russia, and sometimes when she is late for a lesson, the old mother slips out and gossips with the pupils. What revelations! What merry undignified chuckles! She is delighted to have someone to talk to but suddenly she hears her terrifying daughter outside and slips back shamefacedly into her room.

There are many other Russians on Riga Strand, the remnants of the wealthy patrons of former days. All that they could save from the Revolution they have brought with them but they have no homes or estates to return to; they have to be thankful for a refuge from their own countrymen among a people they have always despised, and to get jobs in Latvia they set themselves to learning Lettish, a language they have always regarded as a servant patois. Life is very hard but they contrive often to be gay and self-confident and outrageous. They still take short cuts across flower-beds if they belong to Jews, and are condescending to Letts at tea-parties. They are ingenious at finding ways to restore their self respect.

There is also a Soviet Commissar holidaying on Riga Strand, but it is unlikely that he will join the crowd that watches the sunset in the evening. He is neither gay nor sociable. Even at meals he talks to no one but gazes intently at his plate of food, frightened to look up in case he should intercept a glance of hate. He is pale with enthusiasm or under-nourishment and he obviously enjoys the fleshpots of Riga Strand.

As the evening grows colder the strand empties, and a group of boys come out of the pinewoods where they have been collecting sticks, and build a bonfire on the shore. The rest of the sand sinks back into the night and they are islanded in the firelight. As the flames bum higher it is easier to see their keen, Jewish faces. They have not yet lost the colours of the Mediterranean, though it may be many generations since their ancestors travelled up from Palestine to the shores of the Baltic. The leaders are a woman with loose black hair and a Messianic youth of seventeen. Are they making speeches or telling stories? The eyes of twenty boys are fixed, black and burning in the firelight, on the woman as she cries passionately to them in Yiddish. Three or four boys reply to her and they sing strange, unhomely

— Riga Strand in 1930 —

Eastern tunes. Only a few yards away are the cafes and the sanatoria but in the darkness the sand seems to stretch away interminably and the Jewish scouts seem to be the only creatures alive on the shore, a nomad tribe camping in the desert. They are of the same race, the same families perhaps, as the predatory blondes in the beach costumes, but the spirit that fills them now is alien from Riga or from Europe. Persecution has hardened them and given them strength to survive war and revolution and even to profit by them and direct them. Perhaps it is they in the end who will decide the future of Riga Strand.

At last the fire dies down, the boys make ready for sleep, and once more the small, scarcely audible sounds of the waves break upon the silence.

– Report on Yugoslavia –
[1947]

I spent a part of last summer in Yugoslavia, which I knew well before the war, because I was a teacher in Zagreb and held a travelling scholarship from the school of Slavonic Studies. The Yugoslavs are, like my own nation the Irish, among the least pacifist people in Europe and at the best of times it would not be easy to persuade them that liberty could be won or maintained except by fighting. They have good historical arguments for this view. Serbia, for example, became free after repeated insurrections against the Turks, and the other Slav provinces – Croatia, Slovenia, Bosnia and Herzegovina, and Montenegro – were only added to the Yugoslav state as a result of the Great War. You might argue that Austria-Hungary, through the growth of liberal ideas, and Turkey through indolence, were in any case relaxing their grip on their subjects. You might say that the Yugoslavs could have obtained their freedom by obstructiveness that stopped short of killing, by the development of cultural institutions, by passive resistance and political manoeuvres. You might argue quite plausibly on those lines, but I am afraid you would argue in vain. On the whole, history, as it is ordinarily interpreted, is against the pacifist in the

— *Report on Yugoslavia* —

Balkans. He must depend on faith, on the belief that by following his conscience he will ultimately be justified, even though the facts of everyday life contradict him. Only by great personal courage and high intelligence would a pacifist in Ireland or Yugoslavia win any respect. If he depended on the ordinary arguments of expediency, it would simply be supposed that he was a coward or a traitor, who was anxious to shirk his responsibility to his nation.

I was not surprised to find in Yugoslavia that the small group of people who had been associated with the WRI and other international movements of the kind had more or less dissolved. They had not actually been suppressed but had been voted away as superfluous by extremists within the groups themselves. These had urged their incorporation ('to prevent overlapping' is the usual excuse for this kind of cannibalism) in the officially sponsored societies, the various anti-Fascist leagues, cultural, economic, male and female. I did not find that they had been persecuted so much as rendered powerless. I talked to several men and women who before the war had been active, internationally minded people, who visited conferences all over Europe and America, who were used to lecturing and writing. I think I seemed to them, as would anybody else from our islands, a figure from the past, stirring very sad memories that had scarcely any bearing on the life they were leading. The business of living from one day to the next was absorbing all their energies.

They had often lost their jobs or their incomes and had no surplus leisure for thinking of abstract problems or international movements. All their efforts were bent on securing some sort of future for their children or elderly relatives. 'We are tired of living', one of them told me very sadly.

Most of these people were liberals by temperament, left-wing rather than right, so that their extinction by the Communists is a cruel tragedy. But none of those to whom I talked had gone back on their principles or come to believe in reactionary politics; they still valued individual liberty, the freedom to think and act in the light of reason. Simply they had been robbed of all power to advance their views. I think that an external pacifist organization can make very few demands on these people. Even by communicating with us they come under the suspicion of giving information to foreigners.

You have, I am sure, heard of the trial of Jehovah's Witnesses which took place recently in Zagreb. The principal defendants were sentenced to death, the others to long terms of imprisonment. Owing, it is thought, to petitions from abroad, those sentences were in some cases revised, but there is no doubt the Witnesses had exasperated the Yugoslav government both by their pacifism and by their contact with fellow-believers in other countries. To quote the official report:

They engaged in oral and written propaganda against the People's Republic and harmed the military power and defensive capacity of the country by persuading citizens to shirk conscription. They collected false information on the political and general situation, which they sent abroad, thus presenting a false picture of the state of affairs in Yugoslavia.

The Public Prosecutor declared that these reports of persecutions were sent abroad at the time when Stepinac was discussing 'Intervention'. In this way the Jehovah's Witnesses were linked with the Roman Catholic Church as collaborators in an attempt to defame and overthrow the Yugoslav government. Anyone who is aware of the relations of the Catholic Church and Jehovah's Witnesses will be amused as well as bewildered by this suggestion.

The Jehovah's Witnesses defended themselves with great courage and made no attempt to disguise their views. In the words of the official report of the trial:

They called themselves faithful servants of Christ, to whom earthly life was of no concern. They said that they would not take up arms in case their country was threatened. At the time of the most intensive work for the rehabilitation of their country, they preached utter passivity. Their pacifism benefits international reactionaries whose agents they are.

The Yugoslav Witnesses were principally simple people, shoemakers, sanitary inspectors, mechanics, and they had a simple and fervent creed based on a literal acceptance of the Bible. There is no doubt that it was their simple faith with its rigid rules and curious dogma about the future that has enabled them to keep alive Christian pacifism in Eastern Europe. They are, I believe, almost alone in this field. Not many of us share or could ever share the views of the Witnesses, and we have to ask ourselves how, without their convictions, we can imitate their courage. Like them, we reject all the sophistries by which war is justified by leaders in political and religious life. I think we can do something by the fearless and incessant exposure of these sophistries. Stripped of them, Christianity might recover some of the vigour and universality which it has lost.

When I was in Zagreb I spent several days in the public library looking up the old files of the newspapers that were issued in the occupation period, particularly the Church papers. I wanted to see what resistance, if any, was made by organized Christianity to the ruthless militarism of Pavelitch, the Croat national leader, and his German and Italian patrons; I am afraid the results were disheartening. I did not expect to find outspoken criticism or condemnation in the Church papers because, if it had been published, the papers would certainly have been suppressed. But I was wholly unprepared for the gush of hysterical adulation which was poured forth by almost all the leading clergy upon Pavelitch, who was probably the vilest of all war criminals. He was their saviour against Bolshevism, their champion against the Eastern barbarian and heretic,

— *Report on Yugoslavia* —

the Serb; he was the restorer of their nation and the Christian faith, a veritable hero of olden time.

As I believe that the Christian idiom is still the best in which peace and goodwill can be preached, I found this profoundly disturbing. I doubt now whether it is even wise for us to use the language of Christianity to the Yugoslav till all the vile things which were said and done in the name of Christ have been acknowledged and atoned for. I think the bitter hatred which is felt for the Churches in Yugoslavia is inflamed by all the lies and dissimulation about these things, by the refusal to admit that the Christian Church during the war connived at unspeakable crimes and departed very far from the teaching of Christ.

The principal Church in Croatia is of course the Catholic Church, but I don't think the Christian failure there is attributable to any specifically Catholic disease. There was also a small Protestant community whose published utterances make as horrifying reading today as anything in the Catholic papers. Their disgrace is smaller only because there were fewer of them. The mistake they all made was that they believed that the survival of Christianity depended on the survival of their Churches, and they were prepared to sacrifice truth and charity to an almost unlimited degree if they felt they could forward the interests of their particular confession. Instead of resisting absolutely the rise of nationalist hysteria and hatred, they thought they could guide it into sectarian channels. They believed and said that Hitler and Mussolini and Pavelitch were instruments in the hands of God for the establishment of his Kingdom. Unsatisfactory instruments, perhaps, they might admit among themselves, but God has power to turn Evil into Good. In fact as one reads through these extraordinary papers it becomes clear there was nothing they could not justify by the adroit use of ecclesiastical language. You will not misunderstand me if I say that after reading those papers for several days, certain phrases seemed to be defiled for ever by the use to which they had been put. If we are to make a Christian approach to Yugoslavia, we shall have to eschew ecclesiastical phraseology.

You may think I am exaggerating, so I will explain what I mean. You will know about Pavelitch probably. I have heard him described as a guerrilla leader, and the whole Croatian struggle has been made to appear a wild Balkan affray which does not concern civilized people. It was not so at all. Pavelitch was a professional man of respectable standing in Zagreb, the writer of a couple of books, the editor of newspapers in Austria and Berlin; he considered himself the champion of Western as against Eastern values and his object was to withdraw Croatia from the Yugoslav state and from what the Nazis called '*Balkanismus*'. His heroes and patrons were Hitler and Mussolini, and the cruelty which he practised was copied from Western models, the concentration camps, gas chambers, the Aryan laws, the racialism and wholesale evictions, and much of it came under direct Nazi guidance. Yet he surpassed his teachers. It was a horrible blend of sophistication and savagery. You can imagine what was said of him by the Yugoslavs and you can discount some of it, but even his Fascist allies thought his cruelty in bad taste. Count Ciano, who was not a particularly fastidious person, describes him and his following, in his diary, as 'a gang of cut-throats'. Another Italian diplomat, Curzio Malaparte, in his book *Kaputt,* describes how he visited him in his official capacity and how he found in his study what he took to be a basket of shelled oysters beside him. Pavelitch explained that they were forty pounds of human eyes sent to him by his soldiers who were crusading among the Serbs. There are many similar stories, some of them probably exaggerated, but taken all in all we have a picture of a man and a regime for which no apology can be made. Unfortunately they had their apologists, fervent ones, and where you would least expect to find them, in the Christian Churches. This will not be forgotten within our lifetime in Yugoslavia. When Pavelitch first entered Zagreb in 1941, the Church bells rang and *Te Deums* were proclaimed by the Primate. When he left in 1945, driven out by the Partisans, it was under the floor in the Franciscan monastery in Zagreb that the State Treasure was hid, in the hope of a victorious return. It included boxes of jewellery and gold watches and gold teeth, stripped off the victims of the concentration camps.

— THE INVADER WORE SLIPPERS —

He had managed to gain Church support by saying that Croatia was the '*Antemurale Christianitatis*', once more the bastion of Christianity against the heathen, and whenever he visited a monastery or a convent he was received with enthusiasm and extraordinary reverence. The compliments and speeches which were exchanged on those occasions have been collected and published by the Yugoslav government, but they can be verified, as I did myself in many cases, in the back files of the newspapers in which they were always reported. For Pavelitch was very proud that his work should always be blessed in this way. The most remarkable of all these ovations was the 22-verse ode of the Archbishop of Bosnia, Mgr Sharitch, which was published in several papers in his own diocese and in that of Mgr Stepinac, at Zagreb.

He described how he met and embraced the great Pavelitch in the Cathedral of St Peter's at Rome, and he compared him to Leonidas, the man who never gave way:

> Each of thy days contains a sacrifice and is full of honest work.
> As the sun thou art pure and radiant . . .
> And the freedom is dear to thee as thine own mother.
> For her thou didst stand forth like a giant
> Against all brigands [i.e. the Serbs]
> And against the Jews, who had all the money,
> Who wanted to sell our souls,
> Who built a prison round our name,

— Report on Yugoslavia —

> The miserable traitors.
> Thou art the first standard bearer of our country
> And thou keepest our lives free
> From that hellish Paradise, Marxism,
> From Bolshevism.

And he told how, like King David, he went forth into a strange world, where enemies lay in wait for his soul, yet God protected him.

> God has sent thee strength in foreign parts
> God has crowned thy faith with laurel
> Which will never wither, Hero of Fortune! . . .
> Doctor Ante Pavelitch, the dear name!
> Croatia has in thee a treasure from heaven.
> May the King of Heaven accompany thee,
> Our Golden leader!

Pavelitch's terrible campaign of compulsory conversion of the Orthodox Christians resulted in some of the worst religious massacres in European history. The Churches have denied that the Croatian hierarchy had any responsibility for all this, but unfortunately the complicity of many leading Churchmen is put beyond a doubt by their own printed utterances in their diocesan magazines and religious journals. As you have just heard, Mgr Sharitch applauded Pavelitch's appalling measures against the Jews. As far as I know he got no official reprimand for his behaviour from his superiors. He is in exile and is referred to in the religious press as a victim of Yugoslav and Communist slander and intolerance.

You cannot go very far in Yugoslavia today without coming across traces of these fearful days. I had an introduction from Grace Beaton to a sympathizer with the WRI, a very intelligent barrister. He told me that his three brothers had been murdered in Bosnia, in the course of the conversion campaign. His sister had accepted conversion.

The Church still enjoys immense prestige in Yugoslavia, because it is regarded as the defender of Croatian nationalism and of the bourgeoisie, and it is in fact one of the few channels through which dissatisfaction with the present regime can be expressed with relative impunity. Croatia, though she entered the Yugoslav state joyfully and of her own free will in 1919, did not receive fair treatment from the Serbs and for twenty years the Croats have been discontented. Many now support the Churches for reasons which have nothing to do with Christianity. There is therefore very little likelihood that the Communist Party will risk a direct attack on the Catholic Church. It will try to assimilate by degrees, as it has already tried with some success with the Orthodox Church. In Bulgaria, for example, the head of the Orthodox Church makes frequent complimentary references to the Soviet armies. For some curious reason the Churches in all countries have been much more ready to applaud Soviet soldiers than Soviet civilians. Full use will be made by the Soviets of this strange ecclesiastical partiality.

How will the Churches react to Soviet advances? I think that they will be, on the whole, conciliatory. We can discount the cries of indignation against Communism that are raised in the Churches of western Europe. There is as yet no need for them to be accommodating. More significant is the attitude of Mgr Rittig, the rector of St Mark's, Zagreb, and next to Mgr Stepinac the most prominent prelate in the diocese. He holds a portfolio in the Communist government of Croatia and he gave me a signed statement about the relations of the Communist Party and the Catholic Church. This declaration is very sympathetic to the efforts of the Communists to reach an ecclesiastical settlement. Mgr Rittig has not been disowned or discredited by the Vatican, and therefore I must assume that his policy of trying to work in with the Communists and obtain from them what concessions he can has the approval of Rome. So, whether the Church defeats Communism or is assimilated by it, it has a strong hope of survival as an institution. The Church has been called by Marxists 'the opiate of the people'. The hardships and discontent of many subjects of the Soviets are very great and it may well appear to their rulers that an opiate against the sufferings of this world, if it is administered by a state Church, might forestall an outbreak of rebellion. Therefore the Church is not likely to jeopardize its hope of recognition by espousing views which, like those of the pacifists, are equally unpopular with Communists and anti-Communists.

Because of this, the prospects of disseminating pacifist opinions in Yugoslavia by direct methods are poor. You can only act through individuals or through groups. The individual pacifists, as I have shown, are hopelessly crushed and the smallest gesture on their part towards international pacifism would be regarded as sabotaging the war-potential and entertaining relations with foreign reactionaries. On the other hand, the only independent institutions are the Churches and they are likely to irritate the Communists by aiding pacifism. On this subject, I had an interesting talk with Herr Franz Zücher, the secretary of Jehovah's Witnesses at Berne, the location of the international centre to which the reports about the persecution of Christians are said to have been sent. He informed me that the trial of the Witnesses had been the result of a pact between the Catholic Church and the Communists and, if you read the Jehovah's Witnesses Year Books, you will find the same extraordinary allegations made about their misfortunes in Soviet Russia and Poland.

Is one to believe these things? I don't know. All we know is that great institutions fighting for their lives, fight quite blindly and they are able to ignore all those truths and scruples which an individual finds obvious and inescapable. In Ireland, though we have almost no Communists, there is a vigorous campaign against Communism. Possibly the object of this campaign is

— Report on Yugoslavia —

to invigorate the Church, by proclaiming a common platform on which Protestant and Catholic and all the divided branches of the Church may stand together.

Anyway, at the time of the trial of the Jehovah's Witnesses and their death sentences, full publicity was given to the trial in our press as an instance of Soviet brutality. Very shortly afterwards the Witnesses began campaigning in Southern Ireland and the tables were promptly turned. It was put about that so far from being the victims of Communism, the Witnesses were Communists or crypto-Communists themselves. A few weeks ago *The Irish Times* quoted on its front page from an address by the Catholic Bishop of Cork, denouncing the Witnesses on these grounds and suggesting that the police should take notice of them. *The Irish Times* is the paper of the Protestant minority, and so I wrote to explain the situation, quoting from the Public Prosecutor's speech in the Zagreb trial about the reactionary associations of the Witnesses and the grave damage they were doing to the Communist cause, damage so serious that only death alone could atone for it. *The Irish Times* refused to print this, nor have the Protestant Churches of Ireland done anything to protect this small Protestant sect against obviously sectarian slander. The friendship of Protestant and Catholic in southern Ireland is highly precarious and it may have appeared that it would be unwise to endanger it by telling the truth about an unimportant body like the Witnesses. This tacit collusion between old enemies in

Ireland at the expense of the Witnesses makes it appear possible to me that the same thing happened in Yugoslavia, and that Herr Zücher may not have been far wrong in thinking that Catholics and Communists were at one in regard to this brutal trial.

If there are no direct ways of doing propaganda for resistance to war in Yugoslavia, are there indirect ways? Serbs and Croats approach the problem of peace very differently. The Serbs, like the Russians and the Bulgars, tend to be extremists. When they become pacifists they often renounce not only war but all the other vanities of the world; they withdraw into some closed religious community with which it is hard for outsiders to make contact. It is interesting, all the same, that these groups with their extreme and fixed opinions often get recognition from the government, whereas an individual of more moderate opinions is persecuted. I believe that the small Tolstoyan community near Plovdiv in Bulgaria is still in existence and is tolerated by the Communist government. Yet, on the whole, it is among the Croats rather than among the Serbs that the international pacifist outlook, as we know it in the West, is most likely to be understood.

This sounds a paradox, because the Croats were known as great fighters and formed like the Irish Wild Geese a specially devoted corps famous for their loyalty to the emperor of Austria-Hungary. In spite of that, I would say that militarism is wholly alien to the Croat character, which is supple and imaginative. If anything,

— *Report on Yugoslavia* —

they are too docile, acquiescing from indolence or curiosity in ways of life which their intellect rejects. How was it possible that this clever subtle people tolerated Pavelitch and the Nazis so patiently? Perhaps for a time all the small pomps and ceremonies of the Independent State of Croatia appealed to them, but very soon they saw how ridiculous it was. They are cynics by temperament; certainly they no longer believe in war since it has brought them nothing but unhappiness. I think that many of them vaguely hope though that the Americans and the atom bomb will bring them some sort of painless liberation from their enemies and that they will not be obliged to fight themselves. This opium-dream of miraculous release from Communism will prevent them forming any plans for escaping service in the Communist armies or thinking out pacifist ideas. Yet there have been in the past many distinguished Croats who have been pacifist as well as nationalist. They believed in peaceful evolution and feared the contradictions and absurdities into which the military policy of their leaders might lead them.

The career of Archbishop Stepinac is a wonderful illustration of the twists and turns which an ambitious, rather conventionally minded Croat has had to make in recent years if he was to keep pace with history. His life seems to have been spent in fighting and praying for contradictory causes, and is surely the *reductio ad absurdum* of militarism and its first cousin militant ecclesiasticism. He is a Croat but was born an Austro-Hungarian subject. In the Great War he was conscripted into the Hungarian army and fought against the Italians, the allies of the Serbs. He fought loyally and well and was twice awarded the Medal of Valour. He was taken prisoner with other Croats, he changed sides, joined the Yugoslav Legion and fought for the Serbs against the Austro-Hungarians. Again he fought loyally and well and was awarded the coveted Karageorge Star. Some years later, he became a priest and very soon, with the king's favour, the Archbishop of Zagreb. On the eve of the collapse of the Yugoslav kingdom he remained loyal to the king, issuing an appeal to the Croats to stand by the young King Peter. A few days later Yugoslavia collapsed and he ordered a *Te Deum* in all the churches to celebrate the establishment by Pavelitch of the Independent State of Croatia. He was loyal to Pavelitch, praying for his victory against the Serbs and the remnant of the Yugoslav army, and was awarded by him the Grand Cross of the Order of King Zvonimir 'for exposing both at home and abroad the rebels from the territory of the Independent State of Croatia', that is to say, the Yugoslavs. Pavelitch fell and the Partisans came in and established the Federal Republic. Then, his biographer Count O'Brien tells us, he became a loyal subject of the Communist government. O'Brien angrily declares that the suggestion that he remained a loyal subject of the previous government was purest calumny and in his book he prints a photograph of the archbishop watching a military parade beside the military commander of Zagreb, the Soviet military attaché and the Communist premier of Croatia. In spite of all this, it is curious to find in this book the following anecdote to illustrate the archbishop's humanity and courage. At the height of the religious massacres, he is said to have burst into Pavelitch's room and cried out, 'It is God's command! Thou shalt not kill!', and without another word, says Count O'Brien, he left the Quisling's palace. Almost all these facts are drawn from the official biography of Mgr Stepinac which was published in Ireland, and which Cardinal Spellman laid in a bronze box on the foundation-stone of the new Stepinac Institute in America. Therefore we are expected to admire these swiftly adjustable loyalties and not observe any inconsistencies. Mgr Stepinac was certainly a brave man, but his guiding principle was loyalty to the established authority and its armies. These changed four times during his life and he, too, was obliged to change. I do not know what he meant when he said 'Thou shalt not kill!' I think he really meant: Thou shalt not kill too much!', or, 'Thou shalt not kill except when thou art in uniform and thy victim is, too', or something of the kind. I do not think that qualified advice like this is ever very impressive and I am sure that Pavelitch must have wondered what the archbishop meant.

It is easy to see how Christianity became unpopular in Yugoslavia. I see only two ways in which it can recover its prestige, a bad, safe way and a good, dangerous one. The bad, safe way is by the development of a new Established Church, enjoying certain privileges, in exchange for unqualified support of the State in its wars and political adventures. That is to say, there will be army chaplains attached to Communist regiments, there will be prayers and thanksgivings for victory in return for the right to hold certain views about the next world and the preparation for it, and about sex relations. This development, particularly in a country like Croatia where the Church is strong, seems to me very probable. In the Orthodox Christian regions of the Balkans, it has already taken shape.

The good, dangerous way is so unlikely to be adopted that perhaps you will think me naive even to mention it. It is that the Churches should become pacifist again as they were in the first centuries of Christianity, and that they should no longer demand from the Communists the privileges which come to those who bless armies and pray for victory.

Could this mean that they would meet with the fate of Jehovah's Witnesses? There is always that danger, but if has not deterred the Witnesses. Why should it deter the older Christian communities?

I have heard it argued that it would have eased the lot of pacifists in Yugoslavia and given them status if Christian pacifists in our countries, at the time of the Stepinac trial or earlier, had pressed, not for the archbishop's acquittal, as did many Churches, but for his withdrawal from Yugoslavia by the pope. The Yugo-

— *Report on Yugoslavia* —

slav government had promised not to prosecute if this withdrawal took place. It would have meant the archbishop's freedom and some relaxation of tension. The Vatican, for reasons of prestige, refused to withdraw him. I think that this prestige has been maintained at too great a cost, and that a great part of the cost is being borne by those who are not Catholics and have nothing to gain and everything to lose by the advertisement which has been given to the archbishop's views through this unnecessary martyrdom. Undoubtedly it has deepened the hatred and misunderstanding between East and West. In my country I have heard the trial described by people who took their opinions from the newspapers as a legitimate *casus belli*. Anyone who gave this question any serious attention was looked on as a Communist. Yet surely, without in any way disputing the archbishop's courage or sincerity, we here today must regret that he should be regarded as a leading representative of Christian views or a champion of Christendom. He stands surely for the principle of a state-controlled Church, with its army of chaplains and its readiness to support the state, whatever that state may be in all its military adventures, with prayers and *ovatio* and offerings of money and labour. In fact, he stands for all those things to which we here are most strongly opposed.

Those who resist this idea of a state Church with its army of chaplains will today no doubt be regarded as little better than Communists, but now that the

Communists have succeeded in assimilating some of the Churches, opinion will begin to change. If the unspeakable Pavelitch was able to obtain the prayers of the Churches and chaplains for his regiments of brigands, need we suppose that Communist generals will fail to conciliate the Churches when they wish? I am sure they will not fail.

I am afraid I have told you very little that is encouraging about pacifism in Yugoslavia, yet I believe that there is no nation in the world that longs so ardently for peace. It is still a Christian country but I think that its Churches will provoke wars rather than avert them till they become pacifist. That would be a big revolution but whenever it happened, whether in the East or the West, it would quickly spread. I believe that there is no people with a greater understanding of Christian pacifism than the Slav people, if their enemies and their leaders allowed them to adopt it.

[*Typescript of a report to the War Resisters International Conference, Shewsbury, England, August 1947*]

– The Last Izmerenje –
[1947]

For three days the rain had fallen steadily. When we arrived in Kotor, the top of Lovcen was invisible, and festoons of moist cloud swam across the mountains behind us. Nonetheless, there was a band to meet the boat and a great crowd, and on an iron mooring post a youth was arranging salvoes of welcome. Every now and then there was an enormous bang, and he disappeared in thick white smoke, for explosions are the Dalmatians' favourite way of celebrating great occasions, and today was a feast day in both the Catholic and Greek Churches. It was Easter Day for the Orthodox, while for the Catholics it was the feast of St Hosanna, a nun whose mummified body lies below an altar in one of the Kotor churches.

I pushed my way through the crowd, and asked the first likely person I met where the monastery of Grbalj was, and what time the 'izmerenje' was to be. Nobody knew, though I had heard in Belgrade about it three hundred miles away, while here it was only half-an-hour's drive by car. It was not till I had searched the town for information that I found, at last, that I was a day too early. I was rather relieved; perhaps the next day the rain-clouds would have lifted.

— THE INVADER WORE SLIPPERS —

In the afternoon, with two others, I made a half-hearted attempt to drive to Cetinje, but soon after we had passed the old Austrian customs house, at the frontier of Dalmatia and Montenegro, we were in dense fog and the whole panorama of Kotor Bay, which must be one of the loveliest in the world, had disappeared, and we were shivering with cold and damp. We went back; and that evening, when I was having tea in one of the old houses at Dobrota, I was told the story of the Montenegrin blood feud by a lady who had studied law and had attended the trial of Stevo Orlovich in an official capacity.

The Orlovichs and the Bauks were two families living some fifteen miles from Kotor, not in Montenegro itself, but observing the old Montenegrin customs. Two years ago the Orlovichs had made enquiries and learnt that Stjepo Bauk, whose father was dead, would let his sister accept a proposal from Stevo Orlovich. Stevo, thereupon, set out with a group of his relations to make a formal offer, carrying firearms, as was the custom, so as to celebrate the betrothal with the usual explosions. When they reached the Bauks' house, they were told that the offer was refused.

It appeared that an old uncle of the Bauks had been greatly insulted that his permission had not been asked. He had made a row, and Stjepo had given in to him. Stevo Orlovich was outraged and indignant, and whipping out his gun he fired at Stjepo Bauk and hit him in the leg. Bauk fired back and injured Orlovich

— *The Last Ismerenje* —

– there was a scuffle and the Orlovichs took to their heels. A few days later, Stjepo Bauk's leg had to be amputated, and he died. The case was tried in the courts, and Stevo Orlovich was sentenced to three years' imprisonment.

But the Bauks were not in the least pacified by this; they held to the old Montenegrin tradition that blood should be avenged by blood, and the Orlovichs continued to feel uneasy. Near Podgorica, in Montenegro, just such a murder had taken place in 1930, and since then thirty murders have followed it in alternate families, the last one six months ago. It has been impossible for the courts to collect satisfactory evidence; though the relations of the victim in most cases knew the murderer, they would scorn to hand him over to justice. Revenge is a private, not a public, responsibility. But there was a way out, and this the Orlovichs took.

Some ten months ago, when Stevo Orlovich had had the rest of his sentence remitted for good behaviour, twenty-four 'good men' of the Orlovichs called on the Bauks, and asked them to agree to the izmerenje ceremony. The Bauks refused. Five months later, the Orlovichs appealed again, and this time they were granted a day's armistice for every member of the deputation, that is to say, twenty-four. After that they came a third time, and at last the Bauks granted their request. It would be the first izmerenje celebrated in the neighbourhood for more than a generation, and it was this ceremony that I had come to Kotor to see.

— THE INVADER WORE SLIPPERS —

'Of course,' my friend said, 'it won't be nearly as elaborate an affair as it used to be. In the old days the murderer had to crawl on his hands and knees and beg forgiveness; and then he must give a gun to the head of the other family as a token. And then there were the babies at the breast. Seven women of the murderer's family had to come with their seven babies in cradles, and ask the head of the family of the murdered man to be the "kum" or godfather, and he was obliged to accept.

'That shows what size the families were,' she added. 'Today, in all Dobrota, you couldn't find seven babies at the breast, far less in one family.'

The birds were singing next morning at six o'clock, and the fog seemed to have lifted completely from Lovcen. It looked as if the day was to be fine. I was told to be ready on the quay at 7 a.m., and was to share a car with the two judges who had sentenced Orlovich, two local correspondents of a Belgrade paper, and one of the hundred guests invited by Orlovich. This guest was so confident that the ceremony would wait for him that we were an hour late in starting. To get to the monastery of Grbalj you must climb up the slope of Lovcen out of the Boka, and then down again towards Budva on the open sea. Most of the district is a 'polje' or flat space between the mountains, and relatively fertile; the peasant houses are placed for the most part on the rocky, barren slopes, where nothing grows except scrub or wild pomegranates and stunted

— *The Last Ismerenje* —

oak; their farms lie below them in the polje, full of vines, fig-trees, beans and potatoes, market crops that they can sell in Kotor.

The people of Grbalj were always an enterprising community from the time of the great medieval Tsar of Serbia, Dushan; they had their own laws, and the Venetians, when they occupied the Boka and its surroundings, respected the Grbalj Statute, which was only abolished when Dalmatia was seized by Austria after the Napoleonic wars.

We soon saw the monastery perched on a hill on the left – an unexpectedly small, insignificant building, its courtyard black with moving people. The larger half was completely new.

'The old building was raided and burnt by the Montenegrins themselves during the war,' the judge told me. 'They say the Austrians were using it as a store for ammunition. It was rebuilt, and they opened it again last year. There are some twelfth-century frescoes in the end of the chapel, but they're badly damaged by damp, as it was roofless for so long.'

Behind us, a mile or two away, but plainly visible as it lay open on the rocky face of the mountain over against the monastery, was the cluster of houses where the Bauks and the Orlovichs lived. They were large red-tiled farmhouses two or three storeys high, with big windows and several annexes. The Bauks' house was the bigger of the two.

'The Bauks have a dozen families scattered over

the place,' said the judge, 'but the Orlovichs only have two, so I don't know how they'll pay for the dinner; you see, they must bring a hundred of their supporters and the Bauks must bring a hundred of theirs: the Bauks will be the hosts, but the Orlovichs must pay for it all. It may run them into a couple of thousand dinars [about £8]. If either side brings more or less than a hundred, it's a gross insult, and they'll have to start the whole business over again.'

The hundred Orlovich guests were already there when we arrived; outside the wall of the churchyard a group of women and neighbours, whom neither side had invited, were leaning watching. The women, in Montenegrin fashion, had their thick black hair wound across their foreheads in heavy plaits, a black lace veil fell from behind to their shoulders.

There were two long tables stretched out in the courtyard covered with brown paper, but the Orlovichs were most of them sitting upon the wall. The six 'good men' who headed the Orlovich deputation were in the vestry when we arrived, drinking Turkish coffee. One was a fat, pleasant-looking priest in a grey soutane from a neighbouring parish. Two seemed prosperous town relations in smart overcoats, clean-shaven, with gold teeth and Homburg hats; two were well-to-do farmers in full Montenegrin dress, round caps with red crowns embroidered in gold and the black bands that all Montenegrins wear in mourning for the battle of Kossovo, when the Serbians were defeated by the Turks in 1399.

They had red waistcoats with heavy gold embroidery, orange sashes and blue breeches with thick white woollen stockings, and string shoes. The other ninety-four Orlovichs had compromised about their clothes; they nearly all had the caps and some had either the breeches or the waistcoat, but they mostly had an ordinary Sunday coat on top of it. They all had black moustaches, and held either a heavy stick or an umbrella in their hands. I saw one or two men who had both.

One of the journalists from Kotor beckoned me into the church, and introduced me to the priest and a small dark man with terrified eyes who stood beside him.

'That's the murderer,' he told me. 'You are the murderer, Stevo Orlovich, aren't you?' he asked to make certain.

'Yes' – and we shook hands.

We shook hands with his brother, too, an older, solid-looking man. He, too, had received a bullet wound in the leg as he was running away from the Bauks' house. Stevo Orlovich shrank away behind the chapel walls as soon as he could; he was very slightly built, and had black bristly hair and a small Charlie Chaplin moustache; he wore a neat but worn black suit, with a fountain pen clipped in the breast pocket. He was evidently in an agony of shame and embarrassment about the ceremony he was going to have to go through. But he was sufficiently collected to make it clear that he wasn't pleased to see us.

All at once a boy began to toll the three small bells of the chapel, and five or six people went in to hear the priest celebrate the short Easter Mass according to the Greek rite. I saw the correspondent of the Belgrade *Politika* standing beside them leading the responses in a booming voice.

'Christ is risen!'

'Lord, have mercy on us!'

The priest was swinging a censer vigorously, and the whole courtyard was filled with sound and the smell of incense.

It lasted a quarter of an hour. When I came out of the church one of the Orlovichs who was sitting on the seat, cried out, 'Hello, boy!' and I went and sat down beside him. He had been at the copper mines at Butte, Montana, and said that at least ten others present had been there, too. I complimented him on his gorgeous embroidered waistcoat, but he said it was nothing to what they used to have. Times were bad . . .

'Montenegrin mans should do like Irishmans,' he said, 'raise hell, holler!'

Evidently, a good deal of information about Ireland had filtered via Butte, Montana, to Grbalj, because he had a muttered conversation with his neighbour about de Valera and the Lord Mayor who had died after a seventy day hunger-strike.

'I was telling him about the Liberty Irish State,' he said.

The six good men walked out of the churchyard

— *The Last Ismerenje* —

and he said: 'You see that bunch? They go fetch the otha bunch!'

But the six Orlovichs returned alone and another hour passed before down the mountain slope the procession of the Bauks, a long black line like a school crocodile, issued slowly from behind a little wood. They were a long way off still. From the terrace of the priest's house I watched them going down a small lane through an olive grove into the main road, crossing the wooden bridge over a very swift stream then climbing up the hill towards the monastery.

A man came out of the monastery with a big basket of bread and he was followed surprisingly by a sailor with some paper table napkins. Carafes of rakkia were planted at intervals along the table . . . The Orlovichs got up and walked leisurely towards one side of the churchyard, they formed themselves in a long row, fifty abreast, two deep. In the back row towards the end I saw the murderer flatten himself against the wall. He was fingering his fountain pen nervously. His brother was beside him.

The little priest in the grey soutane came bustling out of the church.

'Take off your hats,' he said, and we all did so.

Then the Bauks came in, headed by two handsome elderly priests with black beards, then four other good men.

They lined themselves opposite the Orlovichs, exactly a hundred, with their hats still firmly on, facing a hundred with bare heads. It was like Sir Roger de Coverley.

There was a long silence and then one of the Bauk 'good men', a professor from Kotor, came out into the middle and in a loud voice read the sentence. This is a slightly abbreviated version of what he read:

In the name of Christ the Saviour Who is eternal peace between men.

Today, when the Ascension is near at hand, in the year of Our Lord 1937 in the monastery of the Blessed Virgin of Grbalj good men have met together and pleaded with the families of Bauk and Orlovich to lay aside their blood feud which arose in the month of February 1935.

In the name of God from Whom all true justice proceeds and after long cognition, they pronounced this sentence which shall be executed on the third day of Easter, 1937, in the monastery of the Blessed Virgin of Grbalj.

Seeing that God's justice fell upon the wounds of Stjepo Bauk, the son of Vuk and Stevo Orlovich, the son of Lazo, who remained alive after wounds received, and seeing that Mirko Bauk valiantly forgave the murder of his brother Stjepo and reconciled himself through God and St John with the Orlovichs, we declare this sentence:

1. That the brothers Orlovich wait with a hundred of their people on the Bauks with a hundred of theirs.

2. That the Orlovichs humbly, according to custom (but not carrying firearms), shall approach the Bauks who shall embrace them in this order.

Mirko Bauk, the son of Vuk, shall kiss Stevo Orlovich, the son of Lazo.

— *The Last Ismerenje* —

Vaso Bauk, the son of Rado, shall kiss Ilya Orlovich, the son of Lazo.

3. That at the first baptism of a child of theirs the Orlovichs shall ask Bauk to be godfather and he shall accept.

4. That from this reconciliation everlasting friendships and mutual respect for their mutual honour in word and deed shall proceed and that this blood feud shall be ended for all time.

Each family must receive a copy of this sentence and one must be preserved in the archives of the monastery where this reconciliation was made.

Drawn up by the undersigned: [Here follow the signatures of the six good men of the Bauks and the six good men of the Orlovichs.]

The professor stepped back into the Bauk ranks and put the sentence back into his leather portfolio.

Then one of the Orlovich good men cried out in a voice breaking with emotion:

'Stevo Orlovich!'

The murderer folded his arms across his breast and bending down from the waist he darted forward from the wall. He was like someone in a trance. He did not see where he was going and butted his bowed head into a man in front. It was a second before he had disentangled himself from the overcoat and was heading once more for the Bauks. Mirko Bauk, a fat young man with fair hair and moustache, all in black except for the red crown of his Montenegrin cap, stepped out and raised him up.

'Forgive me!' said Orlovich.

'I forgive you my brother's blood,' Bauk answered and they kissed each other on both cheeks. I heard people sobbing behind me. Then Vaso Bauk, who was small and puny, empraced Ilya Orlovich and finally all the hundred Bauks stepped forward and shook hands and greeted the hundred Orlovichs. Then they all took their seats at the table, the Orlovichs sitting at one table, the Bauks at another. Stevo Orlovich did not appear but stayed in the monastery with his brother.

I and the four men from Kotor were preparing to go home but the Bauk professor pressed us to stay.

'The Orlovichs would like to ask you,' he said, 'but they have to be so humble today – it isn't the custom – so we invite you.'

A table was brought out from the vestry and a red table cloth and we sat by ourselves on the other side of the courtyard.

Before we started to feed, the Bauk priest got up and began an Easter hymn . . . and once more the journalist's big voice filled the courtyard.

A lot of forks arrived and a platter heaped with boiled beef. Someone else explained to me that when the monastery had been rededicated last year, there had been six hundred guests and each had a knife for himself and also a tumbler; but today it was different – it was custom. So there were no tumblers and we pushed round from mouth to mouth, first a big bottle of rakkia, then a big flask of an excellent red wine.

— *The Last Ismerenje* —

'Please you thank you, Mister!' the journalist with the big voice said every time he gave the flask a shove in my direction.

He then muttered very rapidly into my ear a couple of verses of a poem beginning:

My 'ome iz zy ocean
My 'arth iz ze ship!

The meal was quite good and the platters were constantly replenished by the sailor and two men running backward and forward with white napkins held in their teeth. After the beef came boiled ham. Except at our table nobody talked very much. There seemed to be no fraternization between the Bauks and the Orlovichs. First came forgiveness, a little later, perhaps, friendship would follow.

They must have had an extraordinary capacity for keeping the practical and the emotional side of their lives distant for on the slope of the hill their two houses seemed only a few hundred yards apart. Their sheep must graze the same mountains, they must use the same tracks. How had they managed to pass two years so close without lending things and without borrowing things?

There could be no doubt, anyway, that the quarrel had at last been settled. The sentences of the law courts usually leave bitterness and dissatisfaction behind but the ceremony at Grbalj, so impressive and deeply moving, aimed at something far higher. Did it achieve it? I thought so, but couldn't be sure. Did Mirko perhaps look a bit too self-righteous? Does one ever feel very friendly towards people who force on one too abject an apology or towards one's relations who watch it? I think Stevo may go to Butte, Montana.

Most European law is based on compensation and punishment, justice is important, but it is also impersonal. Montenegrin custom on the other hand takes into account forgiveness which English justice ignores, and because of that, when 'izmerenje' passes away, as pass it must, an important element of justice will have gone with it.

The journalist borrowed the copy of the sentence from the monastery achives.

'Meet me in the Café at Kotor,' he said to me, 'and I'll let you have a read of it.'

And we crammed in eleven of us, for some of the Orlovich friends came too, into the car . . . There was some angry tooting behind us and a lemon-coloured sports car thrust past, containing the professor and two of the Bauk 'good men'.

A moment later we were on the main highway to Cetinje, negotiating the hair-pin bends of that incredible road. Every now and then we passed policemen with fixed bayonets and we dodged a charabanc full of German tourists. Below us at Kotor a yacht lay at anchor by the quays, a procession of soldiers was marching through the streets which were green with acacia

— *The Last Ismerenje* —

trees. The grimness of the mountains lay behind us and we were in the twentieth century again.

'It's beautiful,' I said to one of the judges.

'Yes,' he replied, 'but you should have seen it when the King and Mrs Simpson were here. The evening they arrived all the bay from Tivat to Kotor was illuminated – bonfires and petrol. It was wonderful. One of the bonfires set alight to some dry grass where there were some young trees. Not much damage done, but it made a wonderful blaze!'

By the time our car had drawn up at the Town Kafana, the izmerenje at Grbalj was like something that happened in a dream. Will there ever be another one in Montenegro? I can hardly believe it. The 'good men' in the Homburg hats were getting self-conscious about it and I am convinced I heard the murderer and his brother grumbling about the journalists behind the chapel wall. I was glad he didn't know that someone had suggested bringing a film apparatus. Nowadays, too, one can always interrupt blood feuds by going to Butte, Montana.

– The Invader Wore Slippers –
[1950]

During the war, we in Ireland heard much of the jackboot and how we should be trampled beneath it, if Britain's protection failed us. We thought we could meet this challenge as well as any other small nation, and looking into the future, our imagination, fed on the daily press, showed us a technicolour picture of barbarity and heroism.

It never occurred to us that for ninety per cent of the population the moral problems of an occupation would be small and squalid. Acting under pressure we should often have to choose between two courses of action, both inglorious. And, if there was moral integrity about our choice, it certainly would not get into the headlines.

We did not ask ourselves: 'Supposing the invaded wears not jackboots but carpet slippers or patent leather pumps, how will I behave, and the respectable Xs, the patriotic Ys and the pious Zs?' How could we? The newspapers only told us about the jackboots.

The newspapers have by this time worked the subject of resistance to the Nazis to death. They have passed on to livelier issues, so it is possible to anatomize this now dessicated topic in a quite callous way.

— *The Invader Wore Slippers* —

We can forget about the heroic or villainous minority or those other irreconcilables who adhered to some uncompromising political or religious creed. We can look at the ordinary people, the Xs, the Ys and the Zs, about whom there is a mass of documentation. By a little careful analogy and substitution we can see ourselves, and a picture of our home under occupation emerges with moderate clarity. It is more like an X-ray photo than a war film. It is quite unglamorous and perhaps it is only by the trained mind that the darker shadows can be interpreted.

In totalitarian war human nature is reduced to its simplest terms and a skilled invader can predict with fair accuracy the behaviour of the respectable Xs, the patriotic Ys, the pious Zs. Of course there are innumerable divagations but in an avalanche it is the valleys and the riverbeds that count, the hundred thousand cart tracks can be disregarded.

I know that we Irish were not more complex than anyone else and that our percentages of Xs, Ys, and Zs were about average and known to every likely invader. And I dismissed as inapplicable to us the propaganda stories of the jackboot with which the allies tried to shake our neutrality. We did not, I thought, like most of the Slav regions, belong to the area of German colonization in which extermination and spiritual enslavement would be practised. And it seemed to me that the respectable Xs who told us the reverse were speaking either without reflection or with concealed motives. It was surprising when the inevitable volte-face came after the war. The people who had been threatening us with the jackboot in places where no sensible invader would dream of using it, began to applaud his restraint. Indulgent things were said of generals, even jackbooted ones like von Manstein, 'who simply did their duty', and Rommel's biography was widely read in those pleasant Dublin suburbs where the Xs live.

It seems to me that we civilian Irish, finding indulgence where we had been led to expect violence, might easily have been tricked into easy-going collaboration. Yet small peoples should become specialists in the art of non-cooperation with tyranny. It is the only role we can play when the great powers clash, and we are hopelessly untrained in it.

Careful observation of precedent and analogy is the first need. This can be done best in small circumscribed regions, whose characters are fairly homogeneous. I found three such occupied zones within my reach, where the tactics of the invader with the Xs, Ys and Zs severally were displayed as on a small diagram which could be indefinitely enlarged. There were the Channel Islands where the respectable Xs were in the majority, Brittany, where the influence of the romantically patriotic Ys was strong, Croatia, where the Ys were reinforced by the fervently pious Zs.

The policy of the invader in all these places, and the response it met, is best studied in the newspapers of the occupation. Reminiscences of course are helpful but they are usually written by men who are exceptional either for their independence of mind or their complacency. They are edited to flatter the vanity of their compatriots, seldom to chasten it. But the newspapers show the invader at his highly skilled task of manipulating the Xs and Ys and Zs. Reading between the lines you can judge of his success.

I think it was only in Zagreb that I found easy access to the files, though even there I was met with some suspicion and surprise. The reason was that in Zagreb a revolution had taken place which had, temporarily at least, undermined the natural desire of every nation to conceal its weaknesses from itself, or in the smooth phraseology of self-deception, to 'let bygones be bygones'. Somebody before me had been over the files in the university library with faint pencil marks and an incriminating collection of the acta and dicta of the Xs, Ys and Zs had been published.

This had certainly not been done in Rennes, the capital of Brittany. In Jersey there is an excellent museum of the Occupation but it deals with the behaviour of the Germans and not with that of the Jersey people themselves. And in the newspaper room of the British Museum I searched in vain for the Jersey newspapers which were published all through the war, and had to be content with the incomplete Guernsey file, the personal gift of a Guernsey man. This indifference of the British archivist to the history of the Channel Islands under occupation struck me as curious and significant. Has the national mind, like its individual prototype, some Freudian censor, which automatically suppresses what is shameful or embarrassing?

The public does not want a truthful account of occupation. It prefers to switch over from extremes of reprobation to extremes of condonement. You will see what I mean if you read the most authoritative book on the occupation of Jersey by R. C. Maugham. The publisher appears to be about four years behind the author. On the dust-cover the title, 'Jersey under the Jackboot' is illustrated by a big cruel boot crashing down on a helpless little green island and the blurb talks of the 'courage and fortitude of the islanders' and 'the misery, ignominy and privations that marked the trail of the Nazi hordes across the face of Europe'. But the author makes it plain that the islanders were subjected to a more subtle instrument of pressure than the jackboot. They were very liberally treated indeed. The small island parliaments and courts continued to function, provided all their measures were submitted to German sanction. It was by an ordinance of the Guernsey Royal Court that all talk against the Germans was made punishable; thus when the manager of the Rich's stores was cheeky to a German customer, it was before the Guernsey Court that he appeared. He got off by explaining that it was all a mistake, that the German officers had all been charming and his son-in-law was taking German lessons. Divine service with prayers for the Royal family and the Empire were permitted. So were cinemas and newspapers.

In an organized society our dependence on the newspapers is abject. The readers of the *Guernsey Evening Post* were shocked and repelled no doubt to see articles by Goebbels and Lord Haw-Haw, but not to the pitch of stopping their subscriptions. How else could they advertise their cocker spaniels and their lawn mowers or learn about the cricket results? Ultimately Haw-Haw became an accepted feature like the testimonials for digestive pills, and an edge of horror and revulsion was blunted. Here is the printed summary of events for an October day in the first year of the occupation.

'Dog-biscuits made locally. Table-tennis League of Six Teams formed. German orders relating to measures against Jews published. Silver Wedding anniversary of Mr and Mrs W. J. Bird.' The news of the deportation and torture of the local shopkeepers is made more palatable by being sandwiched between sport and domestic pets and society gossip. 'Lady Ozanne had passed a fairly good night.' 'Mr Stephen Candon is as comfortable as can be expected.' There was Roller Skating at St George's Hall and 'Laugh it Off' was still retained at The Regal and 'the bride looked charming in a white georgette frock'. Lubricated by familiar trivialities, the mind glided over what was barbarous and terrible.

The *Herrenvolk* philosophy judiciously applied, as it was in the Channel Islands, can be swallowed easily enough if you have not too sensitive a digestion and belong to a ruling race yourself. Flowerbeds were trampled, housemaids whistled to, garden tools unceremoniously borrowed, but formal apologies, printed receipts were often forthcoming if applied for. 'I must record,' wrote Mr Maugham, of the German soldiers in his garage, 'they did their best to give us as little trouble as possible, were perfectly polite and grateful for any slight help which they received from us,' and the Procurator of Guernsey officially declared: 'The Germans behaved as good soldiers, sans peur et sans reproche.'

Such behaviour is plainly more formidable than the jackboot, we are hypnotized by the correctness of the invader into accepting invasion itself as correct. The solidarity of our resistance is undermined by carefully graded civilities, our social and racial hierarchies are respected. For example in Jersey there were Irish tomato pickers and Russian prisoners at whose expense German prestige was adroitly raised in British eyes. When wireless sets .were confiscated the Irish, with disdainful correctness, were paid for theirs as they were neutrals. This punctiliousness was more repaying than jackboots since it drove a wedge of jealousy between English and Irish. When later on a feud broke out between the 'correct' occupation troops and some 'incorrect' naval ratings who daubed the shop fronts of St Helier with swastikas, the authorities blamed this breach of etiquette upon the Irish, and there were some gentlemanly headshakings between the German and English officials over these vulgar antics of an inferior breed.

I don't think the Germans on the island had a difficult task in making the Russians in Jersey detested. Some of the Russians, who were employed in the fortification of the island, were convicts liberated from prison in the German advance into Russia. They were worked hard, fed little and flogged. A whip that was used on them can be seen in the Jersey Museum. They were inadequately guarded. Almost mad with hunger, they broke loose and pillaged the neat holdings of the Jersey farmers, taking hens, pigs, cabbages, clothes from the line. These raids began through the carelessness of the guards, continued through their connivance and finally had their active encouragement. The guards indicated the eligible premises and exacted a huge percentage of the plunder. When the Jersey people asked for protection they were met with a humorous shrug from the officials. 'Well, they are your allies. Must *we* protect you from them?'

It is hard for the Xs to keep a balanced judgment in such circumstances. Other problems too arise. Should they acknowledge the salute of the amiable Rittmeister, who had known their cousins at Weybridge? Should they turn the other cheek when a degenerate Mongol ally robs the hen-roost? These problems are more disintegrating to the resistance of the Xs than bombs or jackboots, and a competent invader will make them inescapable. In a Zagreb newspaper of 1942, *Deutsche Zeitung in Kroatien*, I read that Ireland, with Croatia and Slovakia, was to be one of the three model 'allied' states in German Europe. In other papers too there was much of flattering intent about the common loyalty of Croats and Irish to Faith and Fatherland, our similar histories, romantic temperaments and literary gifts. Irish plays continued to be played in Zagreb, when English were tabu.

All the same I think that Brittany under the Nazis offers more profitable analogies for us in Ireland than does Croatia. In Brittany the German attempt to exploit the patriotism of the Ys and the piety of the Zs, which in Croatia had been triumphantly successful, was only half-hearted. The Nazis had no doubt of the need to disintegrate Yugoslavia, they were undecided about France. Perhaps, after defeat, France might be won over more easily if her unity was not impaired, perhaps a separatist and Celtic Brittany might slip out of German influence and look westward to Celtic Wales. Also in Brittany the Catholic Church did not support the separatist movement, as it did in Croatia. There was no wide-scale convergence of patriotism and piety. By conciliating the patriotic Ys, the Germans might risk offending the pious Zs.

For all these reasons Nazi policy in Brittany was very inconsistent. The Germans sheltered the Breton rebel leaders, Mordrel and Debauvais, as they had once sheltered Roger Casement and they too were in-

— *The Invader Wore Slippers* —

vited to recruit a rebel army to fight for independence among the prisoners of war. The Breton prisoners responded in the same half-hearted way as the Irish had once done. The Germans, however, continued to support the Breton movement till France had been brought to her knees. Then they made terms with Vichy, withdrew all aid from the Breton separatists and allowed them to operate only against the Maquis. They led the Bretons the sort of dance that cannot be done in jackboots.

I think the Nazi policy in regard to Ireland would have been equally agile and ambiguous. The Celtic nationalist would, as in Brittany, have been regarded as a valuable tool for undermining a non-German hegemony, but of decidedly less value for the reconstruction of a German one. The nationalist would have been manoeuvred, not kicked, out of his privileged position.

Judging by the Breton analogy, I think the first impact of the changed policy might have been borne by the handful of single-minded German Celtophiles, who would have been entrusted with the early stages of the programme. A successfully double-faced policy requires at the start the complicity of many single-minded idealists, native and foreign.

I think when the success of the invasion had been assured, it would have emerged that the respectable Xs, the Anglo-Irish *Herrenvolk* of Ulster and the Dublin suburbs, would prove the more satisfactory accomplices in establishing the German hegemony. The

Jersey treatment would have been applied to them, insofar as they were civilians. There would have been a dazzling display of 'correctness'. It is probable that at Greystones and Newtownards, as at St Helier and at Peterport, divine service with prayers for the King and the British Empire would continue to be permitted in the Protestant churches. Certainly the inevitable bias of German correctness would have been towards the Anglo-Saxon, towards bridge and fox hunting, and away from the Irish, from ceilidhes and hurley matches and language festivals. A master race will be at times indulgent to these regional enthusiasms but will not participate in them. Ultimately this bias would have led to a complete reversal of policy, more in keeping with the *Herrenvolk* philosophy. Lord Haw-Haw, an Irishman himself, seems to have been in closer sympathy with the Mosleyites than with the Irish republicans. The British Naziphiles were romantic, traditional, imperialist. Irish separatism would have been incompatible with their Kiplingesque ideal of a merry, beer-drinking 'old' England, allied with Germany, grasping once more in her strong right hand the reins of empire and dealing out firm justice to the lesser breeds. I do not see how the Irish could have raised themselves permanently into the *Herrenvolk* class from which Czechs and Poles had been excluded. Of course the Croats had arrived there. But they must have felt their position precarious, because two well-known Croatian scholars, Father Shegitch and Professor Butch, developed the theory that the Croats were really Goths who had slipped into a Slav language by some accident. Pavelitch, the 'Leader' of Croatia, who had a private passion for philology, favoured the theory and brought out a Croat lexicon in which all words of Serbian origin were eliminated, a work of great ingenuity because the Serbian and Croatian languages are all but identical. We Irish would inevitably have felt uneasy. There had been in Ireland eminent German Celtic scholars who had not managed to conceal their contempt for the modem representatives of those Celtic peoples whose early history enthralled them. Nazi philosophy was permeated with race snobbery and we are outwardly a rustic and unpretentious people. When a Nazi leader, Ribbentrop, visited Ireland, it was with a Unionist leader, Lord Londonderry, at Newtownards that he stayed. In the Nazi hierarchy of races the Irish would not I think have ranked high.

It is likely that ultimately more attention would have been paid to our piety than to our patriotism. Its pattern is universal and familiar and so more easily faked, whereas patriotism has so many regional variations that no ready-made formula could be devised to fit them all. Many of the pious Zs would have responded to skilful handling. The other day I read in an Irish newspaper the sermon of a well-known preacher. 'The world', he said, 'may one day come to be grateful to Hitler.' He was thinking, of course, of Communism and it was the constant preoccupation of the Nazis that the minds of the pious should always be inflamed with the fear of it. In that way charity and humanity, where they were only superficial, could be skinned away like paint under a blow-lamp. But in the technique of perverting piety it was in the Independent State of Croatia that the Nazis first showed their consummate skill. Pavelitch's Croatia deserves the closest study.

When an incendiary sets a match to respectability, it smoulders malodorously, but piety, like patriotism, goes off like a rocket. The jackboot was worn by the Croats themselves and used so vigorously against the schismatic Serbs that the Germans and the Italians, who had established the little state, were amazed. Pavelitch, the regicide ruler of Croatia, was himself the epitome, the personification, of the extraordinary alliance of religion and crime, which for four years made Croatia the model for all satellite states in German Europe. He was extremely devout, attending Mass every morning with his family in a private chapel built onto his house. He received expressions of devoted loyalty from the leaders of the Churches, including the Orthodox, whose murdered metropolitan had been replaced by a subservient nominee. He gave them medals and enriched their parishes with the plundered property of the schismatics, and he applied the simple creed of One Faith, One Fatherland, with a literalness that makes the heart stand still. It was an equation which had to be solved in blood. Nearly two million Orthodox were offered the alternatives of death or conver-

— *The Invader Wore Slippers* —

sion to the faith of the majority. The protests of the Xs, Ys and *Zs* were scarcely audible.

Yet, as I read the newspaper files in Zagreb, I felt that it was not the human disaster but the damage done to honoured words and thoughts that was most irreparable. The letter and the spirit had been wrested violently apart and a whole vocabulary of Christian goodness had blown inside out like an umbrella in a thunderstorm.

It is easy to illustrate this from the newspapers of a single week in spring 1941. In one Zagreb paper, for example, the king's speech on the bombing of Belgrade was published with appropriate comments on April 10.

'On the morning of Palm Sunday,' he said, 'while children slept their innocent sleep and the church bells were ringing for prayer to God, the German aeroplanes without warning let fall a rain of bombs on this historic town . . .' and the king went on to describe the terror of the women and children, who were machine-gunned as they fled from their homes, by low-flying planes.

The following day the Germans in Panzer divisions arrived in Zagreb. Flags were out in the streets to welcome them and the same paper wrote in solemn phrases: 'God's providence in concord with the resolve of our allies has brought it about that today on the eve of the resurrection of the Son of God our Independent Croatian State is also resurrected . . . all that is right and true in Christianity stands on the side of the Germans'!

When Pavelitch fell, the Zs had to take a third somersault. Words had by then lost all relation to fact and thereafter there was something schizophrenic about the exaggerations of the Croatian Zs and their sympathizers. Rather than admit their horrible inadequacy, they plunged about in contrary directions, sometimes whitewashing Pavelitch, sometimes making him blacker than life.

Many were able to turn head over heels in a quiet, gentlemanly way. For example the Bishop of Djakovo, Dr Akshamovitch, who received the Delegation from the National Peace Council, of which I was a member, in a very friendly way, was a kind old man of whom we already knew a little. Under Pavelitch circulars flowed from his diocesan printing press headed 'Friendly Advice', reminding the Serbs that Jesus had said there was to be one flock and one shepherd and that, as Catholics, they could stay in their homes, improve their properties and educate their children.

When Tito came to power the bishop is said to have invited the Central Committee of the Croatian Communist Patty to lunch. He certainly attended a Peace Meeting in Belgrade. His photograph was printed in the press, as was his speech, in which warm praise was given to Tito. Should one charge him with opportunism? At this range one cannot judge him, but what is clear is that both governments valued his support and profited by it.

In future wars, if there are any, the formulae of corruption will be a little different but the principle will be the same. It may be said that the respectable Xs will only be wooed by the invader if he comes from a capitalist country, but that, if he is Communist, no dangerous flirtations need be feared. I am not so sure. Acquisitive, tenacious, timidly orthodox people are not confined to any class or creed. It is a matter of temperament rather than of social standing or of politics. They have the force of inertia, which all invaders will wish to have on their side. As for piety and patriotism, whether they are deep or superficial, they are ineradicable from the human race. In the long run the modem state, east or west, will try to assimilate the Xs, Ys and Zs, not to exterminate them.

Horace once wrote that the honest man, innocent of crime, could protect himself without Moorish javelins, without his bow or his quiver full of poisoned arrows. But is ordinary innocence enough nowadays or must he cultivate the unseeing eye? Must he not 'mind his own business' like the professional man, or 'simply do his duty and carry out orders' like the soldier, or like the tradesman 'just get on with the job?' (The Channel Island papers are full of cheery synonyms for connivance!) Are we really obliged to admire the armour-plated innocence and respectability of General Rommel, that 'preux chevalier' of the subscription libraries? He concentrated so fiercely on his professional duties that ten years after Hitler came to power he was still able to be ignorant of, and shocked by, the

Jewish extermination policy, by gas-chambers and the destruction of Warsaw. I don't think these questions can be answered unless we isolate them and study them in a small more or less homogeneous area. It is clear that small peoples are used as guinea pigs by the great powers. Experiments are tried out on them which are later applied on a wider scale. Their suffering and their reaction to suffering are studied but only for selfish, imperialistic ends. Should not the results of these experiments be recorded now while the memory is still fresh and accuracy and candour are available? For though such knowledge will not of itself bring us the will or the courage to resist tyranny, it will prevent us from dispersing our strength in fighting against shadows. By learning from which direction the most insidious attacks are likely to come, we may acquire the skill to forestall them.

– In Russia –
[1956/57]

I. A VISIT TO YASNAYA POLYANA

Yasnaya Polyana is one of the famous homes of Europe, like Voltaire's house at Ferney, Goethe's at Weimar, Rousseau's near Chambery, and our own Edgeworthstown. It survives by a mere chance, for it was occupied by the Nazis for forty-five days, and after their withdrawal orders came from High Command that it was to be destroyed. Some motor cyclists arrived to do the job, but time was short, and the Russians pressing on their heels. Though it was set alight in three places, only a couple of armchairs, some doors, floorboards and a bookcase were burnt before the Russian fire hoses were turned upon the house. Though about a hundred articles were looted, the loss was not a serious one, for at the time of the German invasion all the major treasures had been removed to Tomsk in Siberia, and they have now been replaced.

The house and property have had a complex history since the Revolution in 1917. The early years of the struggle for its preservation have been described with great candour and detail by Tolstoy's youngest daughter, Alexandra, who for five years dedicated herself to the task of preserving Tolstoy's home, defending his reputation, his ideals and social and educational enterprises, and securing the continued publication of his works.

Her book ends in defeat, for she gave up the Russian part of the struggle in 1922 and left for Japan and America. Yet her story is mainly concerned with personal disappointments and betrayals and day-to-day frustrations. The Tolstoy family could not today be wholly dissatisfied with the course of events. Tolstoy's position as the greatest and most widely read of Russian novelists seems to be firmly established and, though Tolstoyanism as a creed is dead in Russia, it was moribund long before the Revolution. It is impossible to believe that so great a genius as Tolstoy does not still exercise a powerful influence in unexpected ways and places.

Certainly I have never seen a national shrine preserved with greater taste and reverence than Tolstoy's two homes, his town house in Moscow and this country house near Tula, two-hundred kilometres south of Moscow. In both cases the caretakers are enthusiasts; one of them, Mr Loshchinin, has written a book about Tolstoy's early life. As far as the dead can speak through the books they read, the houses they built and furnished, the trees they planted, the places they loved, Tolstoy and his family are allowed to say their say without any tendentious interruptions.

Yasnaya Polyana is not as large or grand a country house as one might have expected. In the 1850s there was a big central block with two wings, but when Tolstoy was soldiering in the Crimea he wrote home to his brother-in-law, who was minding the estate, that he wanted funds to start a soldiers' magazine. 'Sell something, please, to raise about £5,000!' So without more ado the brother-in-law sold the central block and a neighbouring landowner carted away stones and woodwork to his estate. Tolstoy heard of this surprising decision with dismay. He had not even the soldiers' magazine to console him for the government forbade its publication. Tolstoy erected a commemorative stone on the site and planted elm trees round it. As an old man he would sometimes point out one of the upper branches to his guests: 'I was bom up there in those twigs.' As his family grew up he twice enlarged one of the wings, and the house is now as it was when he died.

Apart from the final outrage, the Germans seem to have behaved with moderate propriety. The trees were not cut and an ancient elm, called the Tree of the Poor (because the peasants used to come there to tell Tolstoy of their troubles), still stands outside the front door; the old iron bell which summoned the Tolstoys to their meals is now half-embedded in its trunk. Tolstoy's grave, in a far corner of the woods, was not desecrated except insofar as the Germans buried their dead beside him. (The indignant Russians have disinterred them.)

The continuity of tradition has scarcely been

interrupted. Here, for example, is the room, an old store-room with hooks for hanging hams on, which Tolstoy converted into a study where he started *War and Peace* and completed *Resurrection*. And it was in an upstairs room that he finished *War and Peace,* as always weaving into his stories many of the familiar features of his home. It was under one of the big oaks in a grove behind the house that Kitty and Levin sheltered from a thunderstorm, and the Prospekt, the avenue that runs from the village to the house, is the same Prospekt that occurs in the novel. It was the occasion of an unfortunate misunderstanding between the steward and his employer, the old prince, who shared the peculiar autocratic-democratic views of Tolstoy's grandfather, Prince Volkonsky, and indeed of Tolstoy himself. One day the prince remarked to the steward that the Prospekt had been cleared of snow. The steward, gratified that the prince had observed it, explained with modest self-satisfaction that he had cleared it because one of the Tsar's ministers was coming to dinner. 'What!' the prince had exclaimed. 'You will not clear the snow for my wife and daughters, but you will clear it for a minister? What do I care about ministers? Put the snow back again!' And the snow was put back on the Prospekt.

We were shown the hut below the orchard and the Wedge Grove (so called because paths radiate from the centre, dividing it into eight wedge-shaped segments) where the coachman lived. He had been roused up

— *In Russia* —

that October evening in 1910 to drive Tolstoy, accompanied by his doctor and close friend Makovitzky, to escape forever from that aristocratic existence that had become intolerable to him. Surely it was the most ill-timed and uncomfortable act of literary escapism that has ever happened. They did not get farther than the railway station, and a couple of weeks later Tolstoy's body was brought back to Yasnaya Polyana and given, as he wished, a pauper's burial.

The second wing of the old house was used by Tolstoy and his daughter as a school, and is now a museum with many fascinating family portraits and photographs. I saw there the photographs of Tolstoy's funeral which was attended by all the peasants for miles around. All the birch trees round the grave were black with boys and men, perched in the branches to see the burial.

There is an upper room in which the old man lay ill for a long period. There is a striped armchair, and on the iron bed a gaudy bedspread embroidered by Countess Tolstoy. Above it is a photograph of Tolstoy sitting on the same bedspread, on the same bed, talking to Dr Makovitzky who is sitting in the same striped armchair. Beside it is another extant memorial of the past, a frightful leather cushion presented by the municipality of Tula and stamped with its compliments in gilt; it has survived the revolution and the Nazi occupation.

When we left Mr Loshchinin gave us each a green

Antonovsky apple from the orchard but he scrupulously disclaimed for it an unblemished Tolstoyan heredity. The Antonovskies which Tolstoy had planted had died in the frost of 1948, and these were replacements. The great birch trees on the Prospekt had also died and been replaced, regrettably enough, by gloomy conifers.

I expect Mr Loshchinin's Antonovskies taste much the same as Tolstoy's, but the flavour of Tolstoyanism and the circumstances which produced it are harder to recapture. Yet, Mr Loshchinin and his colleagues (I was told that Tolstoy's last secretary still works in the museum, but he was absent when I was there) have done their best. And, if one is to believe that the past can ever be satisfactorily potted for posterity, it can seldom have been done with greater care and conscientiousness than at Yasnaya Polyana.

II. SIBERIAN JOURNEY

Though it is more accessible than it has every been, Siberia has never been so little known to us. Forty years ago it was liberally sprinkled with governesses from the West and reports came back to English rectories and Scottish manses about their remote and snow-bound lives. At the time of the Bolshevik Revolution an excitable French minister, who wanted allied intervention from Vladivostock, reported the murder of some fifty French governesses at Irkutsk, a frontier town on the edges of Mongolia. Unfortunately for his plans the governesses had not been murdered at all, and perhaps he had exaggerated their numbers also; as the French are reluctant travellers it would be sufficiently extraordinary if even ten French governesses had ever reached the pink shores of Lake Baikal. In the struggle for cultural supremacy, English, Irish, Scottish governesses pressed hard upon the French and had the Revolution not happened it is likely that English rather than French would have become the drawing-room language of the Russian upper classes. There must have been many English teachers in Siberia.

Nowadays few of us see anything of Siberia but its airports; we accomplish in a couple of days vast journeys which up till recently took several weeks, and as we grumble a good deal about sleepless nights it is wholesome to read of Anton Chekhov's journey across Siberia in 1890. We passed great cities without noticing them, while in his mind small villages were to be indelibly engraved. Here he spent the night in the ferryman's hut waiting for the storm to abate so that he could cross the Irtish; his sodden felt boots were turning to gelatine on the stove. Here his buggy crashed into the post waggon and he was hurled onto the ground with his portmanteau on top. But there were no such landmarks for our journey. Even the airports are inextricably confused. Was it at Sverdlovsk that we ordered omelette and got fried eggs, and was Sverdlovsk the new name for Ekaterinburg where the imperial family were murdered in 1918? Yes, I think it was, and I know it was at Omsk that mud prevented us reaching the airport buildings and some peasants told us that it was the centre of vast state-owned farms as distinct from collectives. But I cannot be sure whether it was at Novosibirsk, the greatest city in Siberia, that we saw the jet plane that is to do the journey from Moscow to Peking in eight hours and the little garden of frost-bitten asters encircling a marble Lenin sitting on a marble sofa and patting paternally the marble shoulders of Stalin. In general one Brobdignagian air palace was much like the next; heavy plush curtains divided the saloons and the cavities between the Corinthian columns were draped and decorated with epic gentility. There were chrysanthemums girdled with paper lace, tubs of castor-oil plants swathed in velour – even the wooden chairs had canvas covers. There were pictures five feet by ten feet of local heroes of the Revolution, of dying horses, wild duck and melons. At Kazan one big wall had a mural of Lenin, the boy from Simbirsk, heading a students' rebellion at Kazan University.

I regretted that so few now try to penetrate behind these imposing facades. Life could hardly be drearier for a teacher of English in Novosibirsk than it was for these Edwardian rectory girls whom fate had stranded in some isolated manor house beside the Kama or the Ob, but we are more poor-spirited than they were. It would not be necessary to be a Communist to have such a job and one would learn something of these formidable people who present such a challenge to us and whom we fear so much.

Sometimes a traveller after poking his nose into one of these teeming cities brings back a report of dreariness, overwork, dowdiness, provincialism. But it tells us nothing because it has always been like that. Chekhov sent back just such reports, but horror was blended with love. Of Siberia he wrote:

The people here would make you shudder. They have high cheekbones, protruding foreheads, tiny eyes, gigantic fists. They are born in the local iron foundries; it's a mechanic, not a midwife, who officiates . . . The cabs are inconceivably squalid, damp, filthy, spring-less and the horses' hooves are stuck onto their spindly front feet in an astounding way. Here, I'll draw it for you . . . And, O Lord, that sausage in Tyumen! When you stuck your teeth into it, it lets out a fearful puff, just as if you went into the stable when the coachman was unwinding his puttees. And when you began to chew it, it was like sticking your teeth into a tar-smeared dog's tail.

But another day he writes:

My God! How rich Russia is in good people! If it were not for the cold which deprives Siberia of summer, and were it not for the officials who corrupt the peasants and exiles, Siberia would be the very richest and happiest of lands.

At Irkutsk on the return journey fog delayed the plane for eight hours, and at last the opportunity arrived for pushing through the plush curtains into Siberia. We were a long way from the town and a taxi was impossibly expensive, so we considered hitch-hiking. One of us got a lift from some workmen carrying sand to a great Orthodox monastery which is now a cinema. They stood him a drink and exchanged friendly remarks in sign language. We two who remained were overtaken by an official from the airport who offered to help us with a difficult bus route to the town. It was a crowded factory workers' bus. The first frost had come and the passengers were swollen to twice their normal size with sheepskin shubas and padded jackets. At every pothole those who stood collapsed into their neighbours' laps with cheerful cries of dismay.

Irkutsk is a town of 300,000 inhabitants, and if my description is depressing I have to record that though the town and the river Angara which traverses it and the grey sky might all have been made in corrugated asbestos sheeting at the foundry, the people were human and friendly. A great deal should be forgiven to those who have to live in Irkutsk and I record as a fact, not an accusation, that all the women who have graduated (and it is not I think unconnected with a university degree) from being female bundles in gum boots, head scarves and padded bodices like life-belts, all wore vertical tam-o'-shanters with a small feather in them. You will meet this hat all the way from the Pacific to the Ural mountains and beyond.

There was a touch of the iron foundry about our

airport friend Mr Kardin. He wanted to impress us with the progressiveness of Irkutsk, and those who lagged behind schedule; the ancient female bundle, for example, who was moving leaves about with a broom and did not leap out of our way nimbly enough, got a good hammering. But he indulged our less progressive tastes in a friendly way. He showed us the bronze plaque of Chekhov, bearded and pince-nezed, which still decorates the wall of the hotel he stayed in. He showed us the theatre where classical plays are acted: Lermontov, Ostrovsky and Sheridan were billed. 'Sheridan was an Irishman,' I said. 'Oh, yes we know quite a lot about Ireland in Irkutsk,' he answered. 'We do Irish history after the fifth class. We had two Irish films here lately. One was called "The Road to Freedom", the other "The School of Hatred".' I had not heard of either of them, but the first sounded as if it was about the Desmond Rising, the second – was it Russian, English, American? – was 'about an Irish boy, who was taught in an English school to hate Ireland'. These themes seemed unsuitable enough for Irkutsk but were they more so than Sheridan's eighteenth-century gallantries, than Lermontov's Byronic tragedies – than Ostrovsky, who wrote about the amours of wealthy Moscow merchants?

'We must hurry', said Mr Kardin, 'or the football match between Irkutsk and Angarsk will be over.'

On our way to the football ground we passed the bleak-looking Park of the Paris Commune, and down by the cold grey Angara we saw the baroque palace of the former governor of Irkutsk. It has a placard to commemorate a famous siege, when a group of local Bolsheviks had held it against some White generals in the first years of the Revolution. In the same street there was a row of low and charming houses made of elaborately carved wood. Mr Kardin could not share our admiration for them, and said they were shortly to be replaced by fine modern flats. But he had no prejudice against the past, and confessed that he greatly admired a gorgeous cocoa-coloured villa with turrets and gazebos – a vision from the Arabian Nights, which a timber salesman of the last century had built himself and which is now an old people's home.

The many-tiered gateway to the football ground was also vaguely Arabian and had half-hearted minarets from which the grey paint was flaking off. The short avenue that led to it was lined with framed posters praising the cult of the body and urging application to sport. One of them was a quotation from Lenin, who was not noted for athletic powers. The soccer match was already half over when we reached the playing-field, but there was only a handful of middle-aged peasants and factory workers watching the game from some wooden benches. Nobody cheered or exclaimed, and on the opposite side of the field twenty or thirty young men and women in shorts actually had their backs to what was going on. They were working their arms and legs rhythmically up and down and

— In Russia —

sideways, and were obviously addicts of some rival cult of the body.

Behind them a tall row of buildings closed in the field. Reading from left to right, Mr Kardin told us they were the morgue, the boiler house for a vast block of flats and a technological institute. Of Angarsk, from which the visiting team had come, he told us that six years ago it had been a wooded valley on either side of the Angara, but now it has a population of 120,000. Petrol is made from coal there and nearby, at Bratsk, is the largest hydroelectric factory in the world. The match went cheerlessly on and it seemed to us that the players were as bored as we were. If it was Dr Arnold of Rugby who invented compulsory games, I could not wish a better punishment for him than to be an everlasting spectator of the match between Irkutsk and Angarsk.

Some way off I saw the bulbous dome of a cathedral on a hill and I suggested to Mr Kardin that we should visit it. He smiled at this strange caprice but came with us willingly enough up the rough cobbled road that led to it. It was closed and empty except for the inevitable old woman with the broom who pottered about in the porch. Mr Kardin gave her a few brisk words of command and she trotted off to look for the key. She soon came back with a group of excited women. They were touchingly pleased to show us the church and led us through chamber after chamber, gorgeous with ikons and murals and candlesticks. It was all in good order and there was a fine ikonostasis. Our admiration obviously gave pleasure and one of the younger women asked with gentle patronage: 'Haven't you any churches where you come from?' They told us that the evening service was just over and that on Sundays the large church was full.

I can well believe this because, on the way from Moscow to Yasnaya Polyana, I had stopped one Sunday morning to see the church in Lopasna, which is now called Chekhov, because Anton Chekhov lived a few miles east of it at Melihovo. The church had been so full that I could scarcely get beyond the door. There, too, the congregation was mainly of women and older men; it is hard to make deductions about the survival of Christianity in Russia because one does not know how many former parishes each church now has to serve. In Irkutsk, apart from the large church which was used as a cinema, the large monastery church which dominates the town from the crest of a hill is now used as a planetarium.

I regretted that I had not been able to visit Melihovo, because Chekhov, though he was an unorthodox Christian and called himself a 'materialist', had given to the local church a gleaming spire which could be seen for miles around. I would like to have seen it if it still survived and if reference was made to it in the Chekhov museum at Melihovo. About Christianity in Russia there is great need for an unemotional record such as Chekhov made of the convict island of Sakhalin. For he not only made a census of the inhabitants but interviewed many hundreds of officials and peasants. Listening to their life-stories he had to reckon the part which fear, dishonesty, simplicity and ambition had played in what they told him. No one had believed that the Tsar's government would permit such a survey to be made by a humanist of unorthodox views. But the unbelievable happened; he had been allowed.

On our way back to the bus Mr Kardin lingered with pride through the main square of Irkutsk, which is like an iron-founder's dream of a university campus. A huge square of scraggy grass is surrounded by vast academies and institutes of scientific research. They wear on their pediments, carved in stone, abrupt, congested titles, such as Vostsibugol, which is short for the Eastern Siberian Coal Research Institute. Among them is a colossal library, a museum, students' hostels. They are vast factories of learning, where moujiks are smelted and hammered into scientists. As on an endless conveyor belt a stream of geologists, mineralogists and plant-physicists passes through these buildings and falls, in a thin spray of professors and engineers, over backward and thinly populated regions of Russia.

The province of Irkutsk is one of the great centres of industrial development in Russia and perhaps in Europe. Every conceivable mineral lies beneath its soil and only the men and machines for mining it and converting it to some higher purpose are absent. More and more of the experts are now bred locally, but the

— THE INVADER WORE SLIPPERS —

working-class populations to fill the great new cities are drafted in from all the regions of Russia.

Sir Eric Ashby, Vice-Chancellor of Queen's University, Belfast, once gave formidable statistics about this great drive for scientific education in Russia. From a population which was 75 per cent illiterate in 1918, so many science teachers and experts are now being trained that they not only satisfy Russia's present needs but can be lent to the backward countries of Asia. In 1954 250,000 science teachers were working in Russia as against 20,000 in Britain.

Walking with Mr Kardin through Irkutsk, one could easily persuade oneself that all this was very regrettable and alarming. Vostsibugol soars above the decaying villas and ugly tenement houses like some sinister intellectual forcing-house from the Brave New World of 1984, that vision of the future with which two disillusioned Etonians have clouded our judgments. But had one seen Irkutsk as Chekhov saw it in 1890, surely one would judge it less harshly? To the grandson of the ferryman who sheltered the writer on the banks of the Irtish, Vostsibugol must seem the gateway into a world of unimagined opportunity; it must offer to his young heart the same glamorous illusions of emancipation that Christchurch or King's holds out to the middle-class youth of England.

Perhaps if one were to spend several months in Irkutsk one might be able to make some sense of this extraordinary jumble of colossal enterprises and mean economies, of generous ambitions and spiritual poverty, of desperate ignorance and brilliant speculation. On the credit side, one would have to note the complete absence of one kind of vulgarity, advertisement-hoardings, beauty queens, comics and film stars, and to analyze the new negative vulgarities which are replacing the old.

Without sharing the lives of these people, one could make no guess where they are going. Is all this vast activity merely a stage on the way to war and universal annihilation or is it a short step towards that world which the heroes of Chekhov so often predicted, when, after two hundred or three hundred years of weary intellectual and spiritual struggle, life will at last be 'unspeakably, amazingly lovely'?

– Mr Pfeffer of Sarajevo –
[1956]

It must have been in the late twenties that the first wave of nostalgia for imperial Austria, its glamour and its grace, swept across the theatre and the screen. Later, it invaded the study and has long given a giddy twist to many serious historical researches. For very many people, whose parents fought against the Hapsburgs, the assassinations at Sarajevo have come to mean the first great irruption of violence into a prosperous and orderly world, the signal for the decay of romance, colour and freedom, the prelude to the crude despotism of the bully and the statistician. In fact, there was never a time when it was harder to enter into the minds of those who saw the Sarajevo assassinations as the dawn of liberty.

But the record of the monuments on the Latinska bridge in Sarajevo shows that there was no simple struggle between poetry and prose, between tradition and anarchy. There was a duel to the death between two rival ideals, one died and the other was stricken with a mortal illness.

The large Austro-Hungarian monument to the Archduke and his wife, with its crowns, columns and marble mourners, stood on the bridge for only two

— Mr Pfeffer of Sarajevo —

years. It was smashed by the Serbs in 1918 and in the presence of an archbishop a tablet was set in its place to the memory of their assassin, Gavrilo Princip, and to the dawn of Yugoslav freedom. At the same time the bones of Princip and his fellow conspirators were collected from the prison cemeteries of Czechoslovakia and lower Austria and given a splendid interment. The tablet stayed there for twenty-four years and then it was torn down and sent to Hitler at Berchtesgaden by one of his loyal generals. After the Germans, Italians, Croat separatists and finally Communists held the bridge. Today Princip's romantic dreams seem scarcely more compatible with the public aspirations of his countrymen than do the ingenious political constructions of imperial Vienna. They are revered, of course, like a historic blunderbuss in a show-case, but they are not for handling.

The real tragedy of Sarajevo was never commemorated on the bridge and yet it was more momentous than the collapse of imperialism or the rapid degradation of the nationalism which superseded it. All through the empire and through Europe there were men of liberal outlook who foresaw the fatal collision and tried in vain to prevent it. Their failure meant the disgrace and finally the extinction of liberalism. If another commemorative monument were ever to be erected on the bridge at Sarajevo it ought to be to Mr Leo Pfeffer, the examining magistrate at the trial of the assassins; a liberal, he defended his creed as stoutly as

Princip and Franz Ferdinand defended theirs and his defeat, too, was symbolic.

It was not till 1934 that Mr Pfeffer, a Croat and a Catholic, brought his manuscript account of the preliminary examination and his comments on it to my friend, Dr Churchin of Zagreb. Churchin was at that time editor of *Nova Evropa*, the only liberal monthly of consequence to be published in the Balkans. He printed the manuscript in instalments and asked my help in preparing an English translation. But it was a bad time. The rise of Hitler made it hard to focus the attention on Mr Pfeffer's scrupulous analysis of these complex distant events or to make them interesting to others. His book is still unpublished.

Mr Pfeffer, an expert in the law of the Austro-Hungarian Empire, tried to administer it with justice and charity. He treated the assassins as what they were, men of honour and principle, who had acted deliberately and did not wish to shift the responsibility for their acts onto the shoulders of others. They resisted the bullying of the police but they were ready to cooperate with Mr Pfeffer, with the result that we have an all but complete picture of the passage of six bombs and four revolvers from Belgrade through the Bosnian highlands to Sarajevo, of the endless variety of men and women who handled them and hid them in cow byres and in reading rooms and under pillows and in loaves of oaten bread, till finally the Heir Apparent lay dead on an iron bed in the governor of Bosnia's palace.

— *Mr Pfeffer of Sarajevo* —

When Mr Pfeffer had ordered the arrest of a student Grabezh, whom he had correctly associated with the assassination, the young man, the son of an Orthodox priest near Sarajevo, was led to him, filthy and soaking and defiant. The police had tried to force him to tell them where he had hidden the bombs he had failed to throw; they had ducked him in the river and in the town drain. Mr Pfeffer spoke to him in his usual way.

I am the examining magistrate and I am going to call you 'thou'; not from any lack of respect but so that we may understand each other better. I do not consider you a common criminal, you acted from political conviction and history will decide whether you were right. But the court must prosecute you for your act. It was not with my knowledge or approval that the police tortured you. If you do not tell me where the bomb was hidden it will explode and injure some innocent person.

Grabezh promptly answered: 'You are the first person who has spoken to me like a human being, so I will tell you.' And half-an-hour later the bomb was found in the earth closet of a hotel belonging to Grabezh's cousin. Another chapter was added to the story of the crime and the chief of police liked Mr Pfeffer even less than before.

If it was due to Mr Pfeffer in the first place that the conspirators were detected, it is also because of him that they remain more than mere names carved in marble or woven into patriotic ballads. We know their

— THE INVADER WORE SLIPPERS —

hesitations as well as their final resolve and in them we see the reflection of an entire nation in revolt.

After the tension and the triumph of the Balkan Wars the Serbs were more proud and prickly than ever and Mr Pfeffer, a Croat, gives a good picture of the small mortifications that the non-German subjects of Franz Josef had to endure. Bosnia, which borders upon Serbia and has a mainly Serbian population had been recently annexed. It was being given railways and hospitals, but every spoonful of jam had its pill and the local Austrian officials often scraped off the jam for themselves. For example, every town had its Beamten-verein, a small club for government clerks, but though the majority of the members were Slav, there was an unwritten law that all the committee should be German. Mr Pfeffer tells how he and some friends managed once to canvass the voters so that the committee of the club was controlled by Slavs and its name altered. This triumph lasted for one month and then all the Slav committee members were transferred to posts in other towns. But the members elected more Slavs to the committee. Then the Germans all withdrew and formed a *Herrenklub* of their own.

If these lofty ways could exasperate a civil servant like Mr Pfeffer, a more violent reaction can be imagined among the Serbian patriots. When the old Emperor Franz Josef came to Sarajevo in 1910, a student called Jeracic decided to kill him. But, touched by his age and frailty, he flung his bomb at the governor of

Bosnia instead, missed, and then killed himself. Jeracic became a great hero, poems were written about him, declamations were made and dozens of students, including Princip himself, swore upon his grave that he would be avenged. The excitement spread to Croatia and four attempts were made upon the life of the governor in Zagreb.

Franz Ferdinand, the Heir-Apparent, was supposed to be mildly Slavophile, and to favour the creation of a trialist monarchy in which Austrians, Hungarians, and Slavs had equal rights. His views made him enemies in Vienna and Budapest but no friends in Bosnia. He was a Hapsburg and that was enough.

The circumstances of his visit to Sarajevo are so strange that Mr Pfeffer raised a doubt that has had frequent echoes and has never been satisfactorily laid to rest. Was the visit a provocation? Did the Vienna Government want some incident to occur that would give an excuse for the subjugation of Serbia? Mr Pfeffer can explain in no other way the absence of police and military from the streets (very strange when you recall that there were manoeuvres on and troops in abundance outside the town). And how was it possible for a second assassin to have another try half-an-hour after the first had failed? The photographs have survived and you can see the archducal car proceeding down an almost empty street. A small boy waves his hat from the quayside, while on the opposite pavement, Mr Pfeffer tells us, six assassins were stationed at intervals (the photographer had marked one of them with a cross), but not a single policeman. Then why ever did the royal visit take place on Vidovdan, a great day of mourning for the defeat of the Serbs by the Turks in the fourteenth century, a defeat which the Serbs had just so triumphantly reversed?

But one must not oversimplify. Of course there may have been some high official who said, 'The Archduke thinks he's so popular with the Serbs, let him find out for himself!' and then cynically relaxed security measures. Baron Bolfras, for example, who accompanied the Archduke, expressed that opinion in his reminiscences. But I doubt whether respectable bureaucrats often consciously plan for assassination. I think, when they want a major blunder made, they delegate authority to some naive and irreproachable subordinate. One can imagine some minor diplomatic personage getting fuddled by the mystique of royalty and Austria's cultural mission to the Balkans. He would specially choose Vidovdan for the visit. 'We must teach Serbs and Turks to forget about these ancient quarrels,' he would argue, 'and to bury the hatchet. We must show them how our royalty moves freely and fearlessly among its subjects. We put our trust in Providence.' Then the assassination would be deemed the violation of the most sacred trust, and the ultimatum to Belgrade would seem to have been countersigned in Heaven. They could settle down to the absorption of Serbia with the easiest of consciences.

— *Mr Pfeffer of Sarajevo* —

As the days passed, the mourning for the royal couple assumed a majesty that must have made it very hard for Mr Pfeffer to keep his head. The royal corpses passed out of the hands of the doctors and the police and lay in state with a hundred tapers blazing. They travelled overland and by sea to Trieste with solemn ceremonies at every halt. Finally, at midnight, they reached Vienna; with torches and muffled drums and a cavalry escort, they were brought to the church of the Hofburg. The next day the old emperor drove up from Schonbrunn to the service while his ministers got ready for the annihilation of Serbia.

Meanwhile in Sarajevo, Mr Pfeffer looking out of his window saw a procession of boys and girls issuing from the police station with a large portrait of the Archduke draped in crape. A wave of mourning was followed by a wave of indignation against the Serbs. Their shops, hotels, reading-rooms were wrecked. The police knew that provided you organize the mourning, there will always be volunteers to carry through the retribution.

Mr Pfeffer slowly pieced together the whole of the story of the assassinations. Very many Serbs in Bosnia and outside it, as well as some Croats and Muslims, were linked in the conspiracy. The individual had set himself in a big way against the state but nothing appeared to prove the complicity of the Serbian Government which the Austrian ultimatum assumed.

There was, of course, a link between the political

intrigues of Belgrade and the young Bosnian rebels, but Pfeffer, after a detailed examination of all the evidence, decided that encouragement from Serbia had been unofficial and half-hearted. Captain Tankoshitch, a hero of the Balkan Wars, had indeed got the bombs for the Bosnian students, when they had come to him in Belgrade, begging his assistance. He was a member of the Black Hand,* a Serbian organization for the liberation of the Southern Slavs of the Austro-Hungarian Empire. It had seemed to him and others that the Archduke's visit and military manoeuvres in Bosnia, which, as Supreme Commander he came to supervise, were sly preliminaries to an attack on Serbia. Possibly, they thought, a bomb or two might warn the Austrians of the resistance they would meet, though the conspirators did not seek the approval of the Serbian Government, which knew nothing of their schemes. Soon after the bombs had been provided, the leaders of the Black Hand had misgivings. Not in their wildest dreams had they thought that the Archduke would be so carelessly guarded that the assassination might succeed, but the young men seemed too ingenuous to be trusted. Sharats, a theological seminarist, was sent post haste to Sarajevo to stop the enterprise, but the bombs were already on the way, the students had

* There are some who now dispute Pfeffer's conclusion, e.g. Joachim Remak, an American professor, who thinks that the whole assassination was organized by Apis (of the Black Hand) in Belgrade, but I don't believe he proves his case at all.

made up their minds. They would not listen to him.

Mr Pfeffer secured abundant photographs. Alone of all the conspirators, the guerrilla Tankoshitch faces the camera with dandified composure, spruce moustachios and a chest crisscrossed with bandoliers. We know the others only from prison photographs. There are about a dozen university students, a village schoolmaster, a prosperous citizen of Tuzla who had opened the first cinema, a patron of gymnastic clubs and reading-rooms. There is a peasant farmer, a very handsome old man in the white tunic and gay woven girdle of the Bosnian highlands. His son, a pastoral figure from the Old Testament, appears with his hands lightly clasped. He is grave, bewildered and yet relaxed, strangely different from the tense figures of the townspeople. You can see in their eyes that their resolution was shaped by text books, newspapers, committees, while for the peasants the tragedy of Vidovdan was the fulfilment of old legends, ancient curses. For them the Archduke must have been a shadowy figure not easily to be distinguished from the Turkish overlords of the past. The bombs which the students brought them slipped into their broad girdles all too naturally.

These bombs must have changed hands twenty times on their way to Sarajevo. Let me describe a single episode, one of many similar ones. One June day a fortnight before the assassination, Chubrilovitch, the young teacher of a church school near the Serbian frontier, was riding beside the village priest to

THE INVADER WORE SLIPPERS

buy lambs. He had offered to help the priest ford a river swollen by the floods, but before they reached it a ploughman came out of the woods to say that two students wanted to see the schoolmaster. As soon as the priest had gone, the students, whom the ploughman had helped across the frontier, crept into the open. They explained that in their rucksacks were bombs for the murder of the Archduke. These would somehow have to be brought to Tuzla, the market town, and left with the cinema proprietor for the next stage of their journey to Sarajevo. The schoolmaster put the bombs into the panniers of his horse and took the students to the large farmhouse of his godfather, Kerovitch. The whole family came in to discuss how to get the bombs to Tuzla. One of the sons of the house had cut his hand scything; he had to go to town to see the doctor; then he remembered that their neighbour had to take out his horse and cart to fetch a trunk belonging to a brother who was leaving his school at Tuzla. When night fell they set off, skirting the village where there were military barracks, sitting at different tables whenever they stopped at taverns, till after many adventures they reached the reading-room over which the cinema proprietor had his flat.

Even so crude a summary may illustrate how the Austrian annexation of Bosnia had brought two worlds into violent collision; it shows that the assassination was not hatched in an anarchist cellar. In the wild barren mountains, which the Turk never completely subdued, the fierce spirit of independence, though it might exchange ballads for reading-rooms, daggers for bombs, was scantily concealed.

Princip and Chabrinovitch, the two students who actually used the weapons on Vidovdan, were reading-room rather than mountain trained. Mr Pfeffer speaks well of their courage and sincerity. When the trial was over the judge called on those prisoners who repented of their crime to stand up. They all stood up except for Princip. When interrogated, he replied that he was sorry that he had robbed some children of their parents and that he had killed the Archduchess, particularly as she was a Czech, but he was not sorry he had killed the Archduke. He had intended to do so. Then Chabrinovitch, confused and ashamed, sat down again. He had changed his mind, he said; he wasn't sorry either for what he had done.

Chabrinovitch was a nineteen-year-old printer. His evidence was heard with difficulty because the cyanide, which he had tried to swallow at the moment of arrest, had burnt his lips. He was a more theatrical type than the others. He longed to be conspicuous and was so unwisely talkative that the other two students, Princip and Grabezh, had separated from him on their journey across the mountains. There had been ructions in the Chabrinovitch household the day before Vidovdan, when he had hidden the imperial standard which his father intended to hang out of the window. He had made his preparations for immortality rather elaborately, getting photographs of himself to present to his friends, consigning his watch and his savings to his sister. After his bomb had missed he had leapt into the river with the cyanide between his teeth. But everything went wrong; the river washed off the cyanide and his terrified friends destroyed his photographs. He died in prison at the moment when Serbia had suffered her greatest defeat.

Their nationalism was of the traditional kind. Princip declared that Serbs and Croats were one people and that Yugoslavia must be united as Italy and Germany had been. They must throw out the Austrians as the Italians had done. They were quite unlike the subsidized revolutionaries of later days; indeed they were always penniless. A week or two before the assassination the director of the academy library had noticed that Princip always read on through the lunch hour; finding that he had no money for food, he offered him some. Princip refused but agreed to earn a few shillings by copying out the minutes of a committee meeting. A couple of months later, when it was discovered who had copied them, the offensive pages were solemnly erased.

Mr Pfeffer wrote his book at a time when the Croats were suffering as much from Serbian despotism as under Austria-Hungary. King Alexander's police surpassed the Austrians in brutality and a Croat might well have been tempted to regret the world of culture and learning destroyed on Vidovdan.

— *Mr Pfeffer of Sarajevo* —

But in Mr Pfeffer's pages we see the empire fading naturally and inevitably as a flower. It could not be saved, but the ground might be got ready for its seeds. Mr Pfeffer and others were doing this, but most of the Austrian officials could not face the truth. Their diplomacy had become a network of lies and tricks in which they strangled as many friends as enemies. We see this happening even in Sarajevo. The Austrians were trying to conciliate the Muslims in Bosnia in order to counterbalance the Croats and Serbs, who formed the majority. Perhaps they had some prevision of their war-time alliance with Turkey. Their Bosnian regiments wore the fez and a hideous Turko-Viennese town hall was erected at Sarajevo. The authorities were therefore displeased when Mr Pfeffer discovered that one of the young men who waited on the quayside with a bomb for the Archduke was a Muslim. He was twice imprisoned and twice escaped with the connivance, Mr Pfeffer was convinced, of the police. He was never brought to trial or charged.

And there were fatuous, place-hunting lies as well as mean, political ones. Contrary to custom, Mr Pfeffer was not asked to be present at the examination of the bodies of the royal pair, but he was expected later to sign the official report testifying to facts he had not seen. He indignantly refused. Later he learnt that he had not been asked in because of his grey suit. In the presence of royalty, even dead royalty, a frock coat is obligatory. Also decorations were to be awarded to all those present on that solemn occasion and his rank did not qualify him for one.

The convicted students were under twenty and, therefore exempted by Austrian law from hanging. But they and most of the others died after a year's imprisonment; Mr Pfeffer does not attribute this very strange fact to Austrian cruelty. TB can, perhaps, account for two out of a dozen. One of them went mad. Is it possible that these unsophisticated people simply sank under the gigantic consequences of what they had done? At times they may have had some intimation of the honour in which they would later be held, but more often they must have thought of the German and Austrian armies advancing everywhere and the Serbians hopelessly crushed. Night and day five soldiers watched over Princip in his cell at Theresienstadt, one in his room, two in the passage, two outside the window. He can never have learnt that the empire he had challenged was collapsing.

The Austrian authorities strongly disapproved of Mr Pfeffer, but he had done his work well and could not be dismissed. With ingenious malice the minister succeeded in transferring him to Tuzla, the home ground of so many of the conspirators whom he had brought to trial. When the war ended, the Tuzla town council pressed for his trial, but the brother of the schoolmaster, Chubrilovitch, who had been hanged, came to his defence and he was allowed to retire into private life.

— *Mr Pfeffer of Sarajevo* —

He was universally detested and yet it was clear that he had acted in the only possible way that an Austrian official could honourably act. He had fixed the guilt clearly and categorically upon individuals who were ready to shoulder it. He had tried to dispel the clouds of dark suspicion and vague accusation from which wars arise. He had localized and isolated a crime at a time when the Austro-Hungarian Government, with the German Empire behind it, was trying to put a whole nation in the dock.

He failed; but in honouring what was generous and self-sacrificing in a young nation which claimed its rights, he upheld better than its own ministers the honour of the doomed old empire which he served.

EPILOGUE

The Sarajevo conspirators were Croats, Serbs and Muslims, and they aimed at a nation in which the diverse peoples of Yugoslavia should live in free and equal union. They were mostly republicans and the movement to which they belonged was not tainted with racialism till the new state was set up under the Serbian king. It was racialism, not nationalism, that undermined Yugoslav unity, but this vital distinction is seldom observed and when 'petty nationalism' is attacked as the source of our troubles, the 'petty nations' seldom defend themselves. Unlike monarchies, empires and Communist states, they have no trade union nor have they developed a common philosophy. They have few arguments to oppose to the universalists and imperialists, who believe that incompatibilities of language and culture are best ironed out by the kindly pressure of a dominant race. In fact, the small peoples often subscribe to this belief themselves. Frequently you will hear an Irish nationalist lamenting the collapse of Austria-Hungary and explaining that Yugoslavia and the other succession states were mere puppet contrivances of the League of Nations, rag-bags of racial oddments, doomed to disintegrate. He ignores that these states all have living languages and often a more distinctive culture, a longer history of independence than our own. And since the Succession States owed their existence to England and France, their citizens often scoffed at Ireland's independence. The Croats used to call themselves 'the Ulster of Yugoslavia' because they considered the Six Counties as progressive as themselves and in equal danger of being absorbed into the peasant economy of a more primitive people.

What then is nationalism and how can it be distinguished from racialism? Thomas Davis, being only half-Irish, is probably a sounder nationalist, more immune from racialism, than Mazzini and the other Victorian apostles of the resurgent peoples. He would have said that a country belongs to the people who were born in it and intend to die there and who make its welfare their chief concern. There is no mention of 'minority rights', because these were assumed. Even in Ireland not many think like that now. Read the speeches reported in the press. Where one man talks of national unity, a hundred will talk of some unity that is racial, confessional or political.

It was because nationalism lacked a philosophy that in the early twenties it began to decay and racialism took its place. The first sign of this degeneration came in 1923, when by the Treaty of Lausanne in exchange for Turks from Europe over a million Greeks were moved from the coast of Asia Minor, where they had lived for three thousand years. This ghastly crime was committed so efficiently under the auspices of the League of Nations that it won universal applause. What Churchill was later to call 'the disentanglement of populations' began to seem a sensible and modern way of solving finally an ancient problem.

The old view that men should enjoy equal rights in the land of their birth began to seem hopelessly out of date, and soon Hitler and Mussolini and Stalin were eliminating causes of friction by large and admirably organized population exchanges in the Tyrol and the Baltic States. The war had hardly started, when it became obvious to all sensible Germans that, if there was ever to be world peace, all conquered peoples should be either Germanized or deported. That much-respected man, Dr Oberlander, who later became Adenauer's Minister for Refugees, said with reference to the Poles: 'It is better to be harsh now than have petty warfare waged for generations.' Soon the contagion of this generous realism reached the Allies, and in 1940 we find Benes writing in *The Nineteenth Century* that three million Sudeten Germans should be 'amicably and under decent human conditions' expelled. When the time came they were expelled. Again, Churchill in 1944 expressed the opinion that expulsion was 'the most lasting and satisfactory method' of dealing with the 7,500,000 Germans of the East. They, too, were satisfactorily expelled.

When we recall such gigantic endeavours, scientifically conducted, to sort out the old rag-bag nations of 1918 into homogeneous states, how petty and parochial seem the dreams of the Sarajevo conspirators, and the poor old League of Nations with its condominiums and Free cities and minority rights! And how more than dead are Davis and Herder and their romantic insistance on Homeland and Nationhood! One has to listen hard to catch the least echo of that extinct ideology. Yet here is one from the most improbable source of all, from Germany, which once led the world in the social science of Disentanglement. It comes from The Exiles' Charter, an appeal for Heimatrecht published on behalf of those 7,500,000 German refugees from the East.

God placed men in their homes. To drive men out of their homes spells spiritual death. We have experienced this fate. Hence we feel called upon to demand that the right to one's home be recognized as one of the basic rights given by God to man.

– The Final Solution –
[1962]

THE FIRST PHASE

When you talk to people about the Eichmann trial, 90 per cent of them (and in Ireland 95 per cent) will say, with some parade of originality: 'Personally, I think it a great pity to rake it all up now. What an opportunity it would have been for the Jews to make a generous gesture!'

There are even eminent Jews like Martin Buber and Gollancz, who, for more complex reasons, disapproved of the trial. Yet if one were to investigate, one would find that a large proportion of these vicariously magnanimous people had at the beginning been sceptical about the extermination camps. What we are asking the Israelis to forgive and forget is not so much Auschwitz and the rest as our own former indifference and incredulity.

I remember, when the film of the liberation of Belsen was shown in Kilkenny after the war, it was considered in very bad taste. Someone wrote to the local paper complaining that the pleasant wholesome film which preceded it (about cowboys or married love) had been spoilt for him by this morbid intrusion of horror propaganda. He suggested that the film director had gathered together a crowd of starving Indians to impersonate the Belsen inmates. No one contradicted him, and the same paper printed a letter complaining, 'As regards the cigarette situation, Kilkenny is a regular Belsen,' together with an announcement that a man had won a prize at a local fancy dress ball as the Beast of Belsen.

In fact, whether you believed it or not, the whole affair was utterly beyond our imaginations. We had to treat it as either a lie or a joke. And this was happening all over Europe. Yet Belsen was one of a score of similar camps and genocide and deportations were practised by no means only on the Jews or by the Germans. They had become quite respectable and might at last have reached ourselves. Himmler was intending to transfer eight and a half million Dutch to East Poland but, because of stomach cramp, was advised by Kersten, his doctor, to postpone this exhausting enterprise. What had Himmler in mind for *us*?

The most effective criticism of the Eichmann trial which I have read is by Hannah Arendt and was published this spring in five long instalments in the *New Yorker*. She blames Ben Gurion for staging the trial as a pageant of horror to floodlight an epoch and the long torment of an ancient people. It was really the trial of a man, and that was how the three very scrupulous judges insisted on treating it, but they were constantly forced to admit evidence that had no conceivable bearing on Eichmann. He had had nothing, for exam-

— *The Final Solution* —

ple, to do with the killing of the Eastern Jews, for this had been a military responsibility and did not require the services of an expert negotiator like Eichmann. Yet when some eloquent survivor of the heroic battles in Poland or Estonia pleaded to be heard, it was very difficult to cut him short.

The trial was undoubtedly a muddle and hard to justify legally, yet Dr Arendt concedes that it had some very notable results. Unprecedented things happened in West Germany as soon as it was known that the trial was impending and that a fresh crop of war criminals were likely to be named in Jerusalem. Baer, the commandant of Auschwitz, was arrested, as were a dozen or more of Eichmann's and Himmler's closest associates who had been quietly working as foresters, printers, lawyers, without even troubling to assume false names. It is true they are being given only small sentences for enormous offences, but at least the reproach of sheltering them was removed from West Germany.

Also the trial disclosed an extraordinary amount of fascinating facts not only about Jews and Germans but about all Europeans and about twentieth-century man.

What was most terrifying about Eichmann was that he was not terrifying at all. Had there been no social cataclysm he might have lived out his days in some quiet German town as the local agent for an oil company. He was immensely ordinary and it was, in Dr Arendt's view, an unfortunate outcome of the Jerusalem trial that he has been presented so stagily as one of the Monsters of All Time. He had had his early schooling in the YMCA. He was and remained an excellent and devoted husband and father, and a loyal and conscientious employee. He had a great sense of propriety. When a young policeman in Jerusalem lent him *Lolita* to entertain him in prison, he returned it coldly after a glance or two: 'A most distasteful book!' He was in no sense a sadist rejoicing in the mass exterminations which he organized. Physical violence made him sick as it did Himmler, who used to shake the nerves of firing squads with his compassionate sighs. The prosecution tried to make out that he had once beaten a Jewish boy to death but there was no real evidence and the charge was dropped.

He spoke of himself continually as 'an idealist' and in the sense that he was not vindictive or particularly greedy, and that he was more concerned with principles than most people are, the word could be applied to him. He said that he had always liked Jews and wished them no harm, and that his mother had Jewish relations. Like all genteel Nazis he strongly disapproved of the coarse Jew-baiting in which vulgarians like Julius Streicher, editor of *Der Stürmer*, indulged.

He went to his death with dignity, refusing the black hood and saying at the foot of the gallows: 'After a short while, gentlemen, we shall all meet again. Such is the fate of all men. Long live Germany! Long live Argentina! Long live Austria! I shall not forget them.'

– *The Final Solution* –

As exit-lines rather clichéd perhaps but respectable. As an agent of evil he was unutterably banal.

Was he a demoniacal anticipation of the Organization Man, that phenomenon of our mechanical civilization that is troubling American sociologists? He had certain traits that suggested this. He was extremely well-adjusted, he was wonderful on committees, knowing the right people to approach and the right 'public image' to present. With the minimum of friction and hysteria he manoeuvred his Jews on to the conveyor belt that bore them to destruction. Their co-operation was, he said, the 'corner-stone' of his work. He wanted to make things as 'palatable' for them as possible, and to be 'fair to both sides'.

It is this aspect of the Jewish tragedy that is hardest to grasp, despite the abundant evidence from every land. The Jews have always had their Gideons and Solomons. If so brilliant a people, practised in survival both by fighting and by diplomacy, could be manoeuvred into collaboration, no people in the world is safe.

It happened by stages. Acting on principle, but adapting it gradually to altered circumstances, millions of respectable men and women, by no means all of them Germans, became accomplices in mass-murder and received right up to the end a measure of 'understanding' from their victims. The Jews, like their persecutors, had the Organization Man's fatal respect for orderliness. They had in 1935 mostly welcomed the Nuremberg Laws, because they seemed to regularize a chaotic situation and guarantee them certain limited rights. They co-operated therefore. Then these rights no longer protected them and they were advised to emigrate. Again they co-operated. The war started, frontiers closed, voluntary emigration became impossible. But new lands were available in Poland and forced evacuation – it was called 'Resettlement' – became necessary. They co-operated. Finally the fourth stage, the *Endlösung* or Final Solution, was reached. By that time they had lost the art of resisting. Jewish policemen rounded them up, Jewish technicians built gas chambers, extracted gold teeth, dug graves. Jews dug them up again to destroy the traces of crime and then were exterminated themselves.

But even this degree of co-operation had its apologists. For example, Chief Rabbi Baeck of Berlin, the leader of the Jewish community and a cultivated sensitive man, believed that Jewish policemen would be 'more gentle and helpful' and 'make the ordeal easier'. And he thought that the deported should not be told the truth since 'living in the expectation of gassing could only be the harder'.

This was not true.

THE ORGANIZATION MAN

Eichmann himself moved only by degrees towards the Final Solution. He never exceeded his orders or treated them cynically. To him 'resettlement', till the

— *The Final Solution* —

Final Solution had been decreed by Hitler in August 1941, had always meant simply resettlement. He had studied the possibilities of Madagascar and of Nisko in Poland and he was, until the end, a great admirer of the Zionists, considering them 'idealists' like himself. They were allowed great freedom of movement and were excused wearing yellow stars. He had read 'the basic books', Herzl's *Der Jüdenstaat* and Bohm's *History of Zionism;* he had learnt a little Hebrew and had accepted an invitation from some Zionists to visit Palestine.

It was in Vienna, 1938 to 1939, that Eichmann, in the interests of the emigration of the Jews, perfected his system of co-operation, which he was later to use again and again for their extermination. It attracted the attention of his superiors; he was made an officer and later rose to the rank of Lieutenant-Colonel. Luck had favoured him at the start. In Vienna he found, as he was to find elsewhere, that the local Nazis had in an excess of zeal imprisoned all the leading Jews. Eichmann promptly let them out and formed them into a Jewish Council and asked them to advise him. After their experiences they were naturally very eager to leave Austria and here was Eichmann ready to help them. He got the head of the Jewish community, Dr Löwenheiz, to write down his 'basic ideas' on emigration and he put Rabbi Murmelstein in charge of the Viennese scheme. Even humble Jews who knew him in those days say he was very friendly, called them 'Mister' and asked them to take a seat. He worked out a plan by which the rich Jews were able to furnish money for the poor Jews to emigrate. To help 'resettlement' he set aside little plots round the city, where the future settlers could practise agriculture. I think the twenty or so members of the Kagran Gruppe who came to Ireland before the war (see 'The Children of Drancy', p.145ff below) may have been lent the small swampy patch of land near Vienna which they tried to cultivate, on Eichmann's orders.

He was a wonderful organizer and negotiator and the Jews, at first, had reason to be pleased with him. If they wished to emigrate, they had had to fill in endless forms and stand in queues at different offices. There were officials to be bribed and insults and humiliations to be endured. Complicated inventories of property and effects had to be made out. Eichmann changed all this by assembling all the necessary offices in the one building and delegating to the Jewish Council the job of collecting in an orderly way all the data about funds and goods and furniture.

The Jews now swept rapidly through the offices, going in at one door full of problems and coming out at the other, stateless and propertyless, but with only one problem: how to get out of Austria. But here again Eifhmann was at hand to help them. He had sent Jewish functionaries abroad to collect the *Vorzeigegeld*, which they needed for their visas, from some Jewish Relief Society. It all ended for him triumphantly. In

— *The Final Solution* —

eight months more than twice as many Jews left Austria as left Germany in the corresponding period, and in eighteen months half the Jewish population had gone. Once in a fit of impatience at some temporary delays he had slapped Dr Löwenheiz in the face. He apologized to him in front of his staff (he was very conscious that with his commission he had become a gentleman), but he reproached himself with his rudeness to the end of his days.

If we accept that he was genuinely attached to his Jewish 'helpers' we get closer to the horrible complexities of human life. Is one to laugh or to cry at the story of Commercial Councillor Berthold Storfer? Abandoning his post on the Viennese Jewish Council, which guaranteed him immunity from deportation, Storfer had gone into hiding. The Gestapo had ferreted him out and sent him to Auschwitz and he had persuaded the commandant to send a telegram to Eichmann appealing for his help. I have regretfully to abridge Eichmann's fascinating account of what happened then.

I said to myself, 'OK. This man has always behaved well. I'll go there myself.' So off I went to Auschwitz and found Storfer in one of the labour gangs. He told me all his grief and sorrow and I said to him, 'Ja, mein lieber guter Storfer, we certainly got it! What rotten luck! But what a silly thing to do to bolt, when you didn't need to! No one can be got out, once he's put in. That's Reichsführer's orders and I can't help you.' Then I asked him how he was and he said couldn't he be let off the work – it was heavy work.

Eichmann went to the commandant but was told that everyone had to work.

So I said, 'OK. I'll make out a chit saying that Storfer has to keep the gravel paths in order with a broom (there were little gravel paths there), and that he has the right to sit down with his broom on one of the benches. Will that be all right, Dr Storfer?' He shook hands and was very pleased and then he was given the broom and sat down on the bench.

It was a great inner joy to me that I could at last see the man with whom I had worked for so many long years and that we could speak with each other.

Thus it happened that, through Eichmann's intervention, Dr Storfer was able to muse on a bench with his broom for six weeks before he was incinerated. This story of Eichmann and his feelings surely has the ring of truth in it.

At his trial everyone must have hoped that Eichmann would stammer and lie and contradict himself, but he never really felt guilty or fully understood what had happened. He had been completely integrated into a criminal society so that the demands it made on him in the name of duty could not be recognized as crime. One could no more shame him than one could convince a faithful old family butler that he was 'a lackey of the bourgeois' and 'a traitor to his class'. Just like the old butler, Eichmann always called his Nazi employers by their formal titles even after they had been hanged. For him Himmler was always 'Der Reichsführer'.

— *The Final Solution* —

The lessons Eichmann learnt in Austria he applied in every other country where a Jewish Council could be established. He told them how many Jews were needed to fill the trains and the Councils made out the lists of deportees, tabulating their property so that it could be easily collected and arranging for them to board the trains. Then when all the smaller people had been gathered and taken away, the Council itself was deported and their property confiscated. They were sent to Theresienstadt, a Czech town from which the Czechs had been evicted. Privileged Jews stayed there 'till overcrowding made thinning out necessary'. It was an entirely self-supporting community. There was a resident Jewish hangman.

In three or four countries it was impossible to form a Jewish Council. In Belgium, for instance, all the prominent Jews who would have been appointed to it had fled before the Occupation, and there was no routine way of registering the 5000 Belgian Jews who remained. The result was that not one of them was deported.

In Holland, by contrast, appalling disaster fell upon the Jews. There was a very strong Dutch Nazi party, and the proud Dutch Jews long established there were confident that it was only the immigrants that the Nazis would dare to attack. A Jewish Council or *Joodsche Raad* was formed to list and assemble the deportees and Jewish police were enlisted to help the Dutch police in rounding them up. The Dutch themselves were brave and kind and as many as 25,000 Jews survived in hiding. But three-quarters of all the Jews living in Holland were killed.

THE DREAMS COLLAPSE

The Nazis discovered that all the states of Europe, except Italy and two small ones (Bulgaria and Denmark), would under pressure accommodate themselves to their racial programme. Save in Romania and the East, one cannot attribute this to anti-Semitism. It is surely an aspect of modem war. As our mechanical weapons multiply, our powers of moral resistance, as though superannuated, become feebler and feebler. When the Maginot Line collapsed it looked for a time as though Eichmann could do what he liked with the French. The French prefer to forget this or there would today be some great monument at the Gare d'Austerlitz to one of the most sickening crimes in which they have ever been implicated. I wrote of this in 'The Children of Drancy' (p.145ff below).

François Mauriac has told how one grey August morning in 1942 his wife had seen crowds of children packed into cattle wagons at the station. There were 4,051 of them between the ages of two and fifteen. They had been seized with their parents in July and kept for four days without food at the Vélodrome d'Hiver. Then their parents were moved to Auschwitz and the children were to follow but there were trans-

— *The Final Solution* —

port difficulties and they were detained for ten days in the camp at Drancy, north of Paris. Compassionate policemen handled them and sad little stories are told by neighbours who heard the children crying every night across the camp. There was a little girl with a bleeding ear who had not been quick enough in removing her earrings when the children and their bags and parcels were being inspected for valuables.

Such stories seem obscene, for has one a right to witness such things and survive? Bus-drivers, engine-drivers and porters were all deeply moved but a dozen trainloads of children rolled on across France and Germany and Poland. No one stopped them. At the end of August the children were incinerated.

Mauriac wrote that an era had ended for him that day at the Gare d'Austerlitz. The dream of a happy future to be attained through science and enlightenment, which the thinkers of the eighteenth century had conceived, had dissolved for ever. Some era certainly should have ended there but which and how? The Nazis who ordered the deportation of the children, the Vichy government which sanctioned it (the authorization came from Laval), were hostile to the dreams of the Enlightenment. On the other hand the Danes, who alone resisted the Nazi racial policy on principle, are often scolded for their prosy devotion to the Age of Reason. The issue is by no means clear.

It was in Hungary that Eichmann achieved his most spectacular successes, and it was here too that he demonstrated most clearly that he was not a monster but merely the well-adjusted child of a monstrous age.

The Hungarians had first of all in 1941 been too impetuous, hurling some thousands of foreign Jews into occupied Russia before the Germans had camps and extermination facilities prepared for them. They had had to take them back into Hungary and kill them themselves.

The next year they had been equally unco-operative, for though the Hungarian government had agreed to the deportation of a further 300,000 refugee Jews, they would not surrender their own 500,000 native Jews, even though Eichmann explained that it would be too costly to set up the elaborate machinery of evacuation for one category of Jew alone. On grounds of economy the purge was postponed for two years. But in March 1944 the Germans occupied Hungary because, with the Red Army approaching through the Carpathians, they feared that Hungary might sue for a separate peace. It is surprising that at such a moment they should have bothered with 'the liquidation of the Jewish problems', but they did. The problem had by now become colossal. Including converted Jews, there were now about 950,000 to be evacuated. The Russians were approaching and everybody knew by now that evacuation meant murder. The Zionists, more realistic than the others, had publicized the truth to the world, and the world was aghast.

But Eichmann knew that his moment had come.

He arrived in Budapest with a large staff of typists and ten officials and he summoned his experts from all the occupied countries. He had expected difficulties but in fact, as he was later to recall, everything went 'like a dream'; the Hungarian police were co-operative and the government friendly and helpful, and most astonishing of all, he had gathered his Jewish Council together in a fortnight and had persuaded a prominent Jewish Privy Councillor, Dr Stern, to act as president. Never before had there been so great an exchange of small courtesies between the murderers and their victims. Typewriters and pictures were wanted to furnish the new office and the transport offices. Herr Novak, who was musical, wanted a piano. Original Watteaus came and eight pianos. Novak laughingly returned seven. 'Gentlemen! Gentlemen! I'm not opening a piano store. I merely want to play the piano.' Eichmann himself visited the Jewish library and the Jewish museum and had constant meetings with Zionists. Even at this stage he appeared to have persuaded himself and others that he wished 'to be fair to both sides'. It was all temporary, he explained.

The vast enterprise, so often repeated, seemed now to be working of its own momentum. There had been conferences in Vienna with the officials of the German State Railways and a new branch line was constructed so that the freight cars could come within a few yards of the crematoria. The personnel at the gas chambers had been quadrupled, so that it was possible to kill about 10,000 every day. Messrs Krupp had their representatives there to salvage able-bodied Jews for their Auschwitz fuse factory. The Reichsbank, the army, the Foreign Office, the mint, industry, everything was geared to the smooth fulfilment of the Führer's tremendous dream.

In two months 147 trains carried 434,351 Jews to Auschwitz, yet by good organization the gas chambers were just able to cope with this vast and sudden influx. In the East the Russians were still advancing but even the German generals could not clear the lines for their retreating armies. They were choked with freight cars carrying Jews.

Yet Eichmann had difficulties. They came not from the Jews, but from one of the SS officials in his own entourage. He had offended against all that Eichmann held most dear, for was not the motto of the SS, 'MY HONOUR IS MY LOYALTY'? Dr Becher, now a prosperous merchant in Bremen, was secretly sabotaging the Führer's dream and Himmler was behind him. Now that the war was going badly it had seemed to Himmler more politic and more profitable to sell Jews to relief committees than to kill them. The compassion of the Allies could be turned into trucks and food and arms for their destruction. But of course the idealists, the Führer and Eichmann, must not know. To mollify Eichmann, just in case he should hear of it, Dr Becher gave him a chauffeur-driven amphibious car. Meanwhile, he was able to sell 1,684 Jews for 1,000 dollars

— *The Final Solution* —

each and had prospects of 20 million Swiss francs from the American Joint Distribution Committee. On behalf of Himmler he had taken over some vast Hungarian-Jewish factories for aeroplanes and bicycles and in return had given the panic-stricken owners free passage to Portugal and some foreign currency.

To Eichmann, when he heard of it, this was all 'Schweinerei' and gross betrayal of the Hungarians who were paying the cost per capita for the deportation and extermination of the Jews and were entitled by agreement to inherit all their property. He was beside himself.

Every day the Russians drew nearer and Hungarians and Germans became progressively more 'moderate' in their views. At last Admiral Horthy, the head of the government, stopped all further deportations and arrangements were made for dismantling the gas chambers. Only Eichmann remained loyal to his Führer and in June 1944 by a clever ruse he got the better of Horthy and, illegally, sent one last transport of 1,500 to Auschwitz.

After that Auschwitz was closed and even Eichmann had to realize that 'ideals' must be abandoned. The tottering Reich was in need of labour. Eichmann promised 50,000 able-bodied Jews and Jewesses, but there were no trains to take them, so in November 1944 he made them walk. The nature of these 'dead marches' need not be described.

When in 13 February 1945 Hungary capitulated

to the British army, less than 160,000 out of nearly a million Hungarian Jews remained alive.

GROUNDS FOR HOPE

Is decency that is unarmed quite helpless in a modern war? I would like to hurry on to the proof that it is not. But the evidence for the other side is still far from complete.

When northern Greece was occupied by the Germans, Eichmann sent two trusted officials to Salonika in February 1943. There were 55,000 Jews there, many of whom had lived in Greece for centuries. Eichmann's two colleagues met with wonderful co-operation from the German military governor, Dr Marten, and soon were able to persuade Chief Rabbi Koretz to gather a Jewish Council. All the Jews were quickly concentrated near the railway station, and within two months the entire community, except the staff of the Council and a few others, had been evacuated to Auschwitz. Dr Marten and the Nazis met with great 'understanding' from the Greeks, and soon after the war he returned there to run a travel agency. He was arrested in 1959 and sentenced to twenty-five years' imprisonment, but as it was feared that his detention might injure the Graeco-German tobacco trade he was immediately released. He now lives in West Germany; he is loyal to his old colleagues and always ready to bear false witness on their behalf. He tried to help Eichmann by testifying

— *The Final Solution* —

that he had saved 20,000 Salonika Jews. This surprised Eichmann considerably as he had never been there.

The Romanians showed even more 'understanding' than the Greeks. Antonescu, the dictator, had, on joining the Axis, initiated such enthusiastic and ill-organized massacres of Jews that Eichmann himself urged the Foreign Office to intervene. The Romanians were proposing to dump 110,000 Jews across the river Bug in German-occupied Russia, where there were as yet no proper facilities for orderly extermination. They had invaded Russia too and begun vast pogroms there, killing 60,000 Jews in Odessa alone. Of their own native Jews they had killed 270,000 without German help, but in such a scandalous and disorderly way, sometimes exposing them on meat-hooks in butchers' shops, that Eichmann decided he must direct the final operations himself. To do this he had to rearrange his entire schedule, for Jewish problems were being settled from west to east and Romanian Jews would normally not have engaged his attention till much later. He persuaded the German railroads to organize transport for a further 200,000 Jews to the extermination camp at Lublin; all was prepared when he learnt that Antonescu had let him down and his labour was for nothing.

No Jews were to be sent to Lublin. Antonescu had hit upon an idea, later to be copied by Himmler in Budapest. He had found that by emigrating Jews to Palestine he could collect thirteen dollars a head from foreign relief committees. Overnight he became a Zionist.

All over Europe people sheltered Jews. Many met anonymous deaths on their behalf and the Jews themselves, in scattered groups, particularly in Poland, fought back courageously. But most men need the stimulus of publicity for their heroism, and courage can be sapped by censoring every evidence of it. The Jewish fighters in the East got neither aid nor recognition from the Allies and the fact that they existed is now an embarrassment to be forgotten, even by the Jews themselves. Terrible reprisals were taken on the whole Jewish community for any act of resistance, so the Jewish Councils, believing that death could be avoided by diplomacy, surrendered their more militant members first for deportation.

As for the Germans, the names of only three German heroes recurred at the Jerusalem trial. There was the Lutheran, Propst Grüber, the Catholic, Dompropst Lichtenberg, and Sergeant Anton Schmidt, the last two of whom were executed. There was no mention of the 'Inner Emigration', those who claimed that they were best able to modify the Nazi movement by taking part in it. Dr Globke, for instance, Under-Secretary of State in the West German Chancery, was once, in his Nazi days, able to defend insulted Czech womanhood. They had been obliged to show nude photographs of themselves before marriage to a German soldier could be licensed. Dr Globke signed a new decree permit-

― *The Final Solution* ―

ting them to wear bathing dresses. He has never had the gratitude that he thinks he deserves.

Miss Arendt believes that by exaggerating the blackness of Eichmann the Jerusalem court managed to bleach the dirty grey background against which he worked. Every social institution was implicated in crime. One instance of this should suffice. Like Krupps and I. G. Farben and many other large firms, Siemens Schückert, the engineers of the Shannon Scheme, set up factories at Auschwitz and Lublin for the employment of slave labour, paying the SS four to six marks a head for them at Ravensbruck. The intention of the camp authorities was to kill by toil. We do not know the figures for Siemens, but Raul Hilberg in *The Destruction of the European Jews* says that about 25,000 Jews out of 35,000 who worked for one of the I. G. Farben plants, died.

Yet one can end this record hopefully. One does not, in fact, have to be as tactful as Dr Globke or as business-like as Messrs Siemen and the Greeks in order to survive and win respect. Proof of this comes from three countries. The Italians and Bulgarians passed anti-Jewish laws but ceaselessly sabotaged them, whereas the Danes resolutely refused to take any part whatever in the campaign against the Jews. The story of Danish resistance cannot be told too often since it proves that a helpless defeated people can, by non-violent action, defend its integrity better than many a powerful military state. The government threatened

— THE INVADER WORE SLIPPERS —

to resign rather than legalize any measures against the Jews, immigrant or native. If the wearing of the yellow star were enforced, the King would be the first to wear it. The Germans accepted this decision until August 1943, when orders came from Hitler himself that all the Jews in Denmark were to be deported.

What happened then was astonishing. The Gerrnan officials, who had lived for some years in Denmark, were themselves infected by the spirit of resistance and even the Jews took heart and courage. The German military commander refused to put troops at the disposal of Dr Best, the German governor, and Best himself showed an amazing lack of zeal. Seeking for a compromise he went to Berlin and secured a promise that all the Jews in Denmark would be sent to the camp for 'privileged Jews' in Theresienstadt.

It was privately arranged that they were to be arrested on 1 October and put on board the ships, which were waiting for them. But a German shipping agent warned the Danish government, and the government warned the leading Jews, who spread the news through the synagogues. All withdrew to hiding-places prepared for them in Danish homes. When the German police called, they found only 477 Jews out of 7,800 at home. Shortly afterwards the Danes used their fishing fleet to transfer them to Sweden and paid the cost of transport (about 100 dollars a head) themselves.

In Bulgaria, as in Denmark, the German officials took their colour from their surroundings. The ambas-

— *The Final Solution* —

sador and his police attaché advised the Foreign Office that the situation was hopeless. The Bulgarians were showing no 'understanding' at all. The Jews next caught the contagion of 'non-co-operation' and when in 1943 Eichmann's agent, Dannecker, arrived in Sofia, he totally failed to form a Jewish Council. He could not even make contact with the Chief Rabbi, who was being sheltered by the Metropolitan, Stephan. Not a single native Jew was departed from Bulgaria.

The example of Denmark and Bulgaria shows that unanimous disapproval, openly expressed, still has power and that in a small country the art of non-co-operation should be studied more than any other branch of civil defence.

Can one argue that in small countries, where anonymity is difficult, the Organization Man cannot operate freely? Either he does not exist, as in simple Bulgaria, or his mechanism is fully understood, as in sophisticated Denmark. Croats, Greeks and Romanians do not fit too well into this pattern, and it is easier to diagnose the vast apathy of the great bourgeois states. Science is partly to blame. Every invention produces a counter-invention and, to match the speed of communication, there are devices for not-knowing which our ancestors never dreamt of. The press and the radio have superseded oral communications and are much easier to control and the committee habit helps by endlessly deferring and delegating. And, of course, the specialist has his sound-proof bolt-hole.

— THE INVADER WORE SLIPPERS —

If one were to choose the three most murderous affabilities of the twentieth century, what would they be? I would give first place to: 'I'm a simple gas-fitter (engine-driver, dentist, nuclear physicist). I do my job and mind my own business.'

Less obvious, perhaps, is: 'I felt so sorry about Einstein (or poor Miss Cohen).' This enables amiable people to swallow their indignation by mincing it up into mouthfuls.

And finally, of course: 'Why rake it all up again? It only makes bad blood.'

– Carl von Ossietzky –
[1964]

Many of the greatest martyrs and saints of modern times will never have their biographies written or their centenaries celebrated. Nobody knows when or how they died. Their lives are often a complex web of insignificant detail which few would have the patience to unravel. Often they have struggled in solitude against mass movements and it is inevitable that the mass media, through which we now obtain the most of our information, should ignore them.

Lately I found a grimy old pamphlet dating from the first years of Hitler. It is called 'The Case of Carl von Ossietzky' and it was the work of fifteen eminent English writers. It is an appeal to the Nobel Peace Prize Committee on behalf of Ossietzky, who was at that time in a German prison.

They wrote: 'We have all tried to do something for the cause of peace, but he has done more than any of us. He has done most of all living men to deserve this acknowledgment from his fellow-men.' Because of these efforts Ossietzky did get his Nobel Prize in 1935, but a year or two later he died reclaiming marshland in Esterwegen prison camp. Nobody really knows about his death.

— THE INVADER WORE SLIPPERS —

Why does nobody care either? Germans of the East and the West are now combing history for evidence that they resisted Hitler but Ossietzky and his friends are seldom mentioned. Very few people talk of the large and honourable resistance to Hitler, which was extinguished before the war began, before Auschwitz was thought of, and which left the German opposition leaderless. The reason for this silence is clear. History is written by survivors and most of those who survived till 1939 had had to make many moral and political adjustments in order to do so. Inevitably they have encouraged us to believe that the best martyrs are diplomatists who balance one tyranny against another and choose (provisionally of course) the least repugnant. Ossietzky, who did not want any tyranny at all, does not fit comfortably into this picture, and so he is honoured neither in the East nor the West. There is much competition to be numbered among those brave Germans who tried to murder Hitler because he was losing the war, but Ossietzky, who opposed Hitler because he was Hitler, and war because it was war, has been almost totally forgotten.

His fifteen sponsors seem rather out-of-date figures too, Aldous Huxley, Gilbert Murray, Rose Macaulay, Norman Angell, Gerald Heard, Bertrand Russell, J. B. Priestley, Leonard and Virginia Woolf to name a few. They all had this in common with Ossietzky: they hated the Organization Man, the mechanical dummy who does what he is told. And they believed he could

— *Carl von Ossietzky* —

be resisted. Nowadays most writers either belong to an organization themselves or else believe that the world created by the Organization Man is so obscene and ludicrous that they can only laugh at it, the bitter laughter of the defeated, of Joyce and Beckett, Albee and Genet and a hundred such others, and with a certain sad satisfaction reflect that this world is a Vale of Tears anyway and we should turn our minds to the next.

Ossietzky was different. He was the son of a Hamburg merchant and had fought with average ability and less than average enthusiasm in the First World War. Even then he had realized where German militarism was tending. As soon as he was demobilized he started a weekly in Hamburg whose aims he describes thus: 'We who are supporters of peace have a duty and a task to point out over and over again that there is nothing heroic in war but that it brings terror and misery to mankind.'

As a result of the German military collapse, there had been a great cultural revival with which the names of Einstein, Thomas and Heinrich Mann, Arnold Zweig, Gropius, Max Reinhardt, Hindemith and Bruno Walter are associated. There was springtime in the air and for a few years all Europe looked to Berlin as it had once looked to Weimar. To Berlin Ossietzky went. He started there the *Nie Wieder Krieg* movement and became editor of the *Weltbühne.* Till the day of his last arrest it was the principal literary organ of resistance, first to the reviving German militarism and then to Hitler.

Weltbühne had been called *Schaubühne* before the war, and was an organ of the theatre. It was connected with a firm that published children's books, *Emil and the Detectives*, translations of *Dr Doolittle* and so on. But soon it was clear that the independence of the actor, the writer, the artist, was about to be threatened and that the *Weltbühne*, the world-stage, required them. The paper changed its name and its character. It became militantly anti-militarist and earned the hatred of the General Staff. For Ossietzky claimed with good reason that some of the generals were lending support to the Black Reichswehr, a secret society, directed against German democracy and defending itself by what were known as the *vehme* murders. He revealed that German commercial aviation was being used as a screen for military activities. He opposed the granting of naturalization papers to Hitler. He attacked those, who, under Nazi pressure, had banned the famous anti-war film, *All Quiet on the Western Front*. 'Today', he wrote, 'German fascism has slain a film. Tomorrow it will be something else . . . Soon only one tune will be permitted, and every one of our steps will be carefully measured.'

Ossietzky was not forced into resistance by violence like the Jews, nor by political theory like the Communists. Rudolf Olden, his friend and lawyer, who was editor of the *Berliner Tageblatt*, explained him as a *Bürger*, a civilian defending the rights of civilians.

The generals were handling Hitler very gently, for

— *Carl von Ossietzky* —

they believed they could use him and had no notion how soon they would be his puppets. Ossietzky, who saw clearly what was happening, had to be silenced. In an action for slander the generals secured his arrest and imprisonment. Yet till Hitler came, a *Bürger* could still count on some justice. Over 42,000 Germans signed an appeal for his release, a brave thing to do for it was only three weeks before Hitler came to power. When for a brief period General Echleicher took over the government Ossietzky was released.

But soon the flames of the burning Reichstag lit up unmistakeably the shape of the future. His colleagues on the *Weltbühne* escaped abroad and Ossietzky's friends urged him to think of his small daughter and to follow them. But he had written: 'The man who is opposing the Government of his own country and who goes across the border, speaks with a hollow voice.'

He refused to leave. The writers of my old pamphlet recall how Socrates was urged by Crito to fly to Thessaly while there was time; it was a duty to his friends, to his family, and Socrates had answered: 'The principles, which I have hitherto honoured and revered, I still honour.'

The day after the Reichstag fire Ossietzky was taken to Spandau Prison and thence to Sonnenburg concentration camp. After that there were a few rumours from fellow-prisoners who escaped of beatings and torture but nothing definite. We know more about Socrates.

Since Ossietzky was the principal leader of the German resistance to Hitler, why is his name so seldom mentioned when the whole German people is being charged with complicity in Hitler's crimes? I've suggested the reason already. It is because Ossietzky and his 42,000 supporters, who were eliminated with him, were absolutists. Hitler to them was an absolute evil, whereas to most of their contemporaries inside and outside Germany, he was only a relative evil. Effective German resistance collapsed with Ossietzky, for only relativists were left. Not only in Germany but all over Europe, millions of intelligent people believed that Hitler could be 'handled', used effectively against the Communists and then, when his work was done, discarded. One must recall that while Ossietzky was in Sonnenburg, the British Ambassador was shooting elk with General Göring, and Ribbentrop was an honoured guest with Lord Londonderry in Co. Down.

The ghost of the relativist delusion still haunts us, corrupting history as it once corrupted politics. When it is finally accepted that Hitler was wholly evil and Stalin's most effective ally, Ossietzky and the thousands who died with him will be remembered again. They were the men who would have saved us – had we supported them – not only from Hitler, but from Stalin as well.

– A Visit to Hesse and Some Thoughts about Princes –
[1968]

T he Butler Society started in 1967 when the sixth Marquess of Ormonde entrusted Kilkenny Castle to a local committee for its preservation. Ours was an attempt to isolate out of world history one small corner, a family, its kinsmen, its neighbours. It soon became clear that the Butlers were no better than any other family, but their records had been well-kept, and it was possible to find kinsmen in France and Germany, in America and Australasia.

Our test-tube approach to the study of the human family has not, perhaps, come up with any startling discoveries. The mere problem of survival of a voluntary community in a world, which has become increasingly regimented and officialized, has absorbed much of our energies. Yet our Society is still young and we know that our approach is the right one. All round us men are rebelling against the civilization of the anthill and wish to be individuals, not units, humans not machines, and are juggling in different ways with the old human constants which are under threat: neighbourhoods, kinships, beliefs, skills, traditions.

This is an old story in Ireland. When I was young I was a disciple of Sir Horace Plunkett, who with

George Russell (AE) covered Ireland with creameries which were to be the nuclei of a new society, co-operative and regional. AE recalled how all the Arts and Sciences had started in small Greek city states the size of an Irish county. But he was an Ulsterman and his visions were anchored pragmatically to Agricultural Credit Banks, and the marketing of butter and eggs. Then Patrick Pearse, a visionary without the ballast of dairy products, translated AE's dream into Gaelic and taught his pupils at St Enda's about an Irish society that was patriarchal, aristocratic, and heroic. His nationalism tottered on the brink of racism.

Douglas Hyde, our first president, tried to mediate between the two groups. He had started the Gaelic League as a sort of purge by which the Irish could be freed from their worship of the second-hand and from that 'ocean of vulgarity with which the British Press is submerging us'. He was non-political and said that no Act of Parliament could recover our nationality for us. 'Ours is the least reading and most unlettered of peoples, our art is distinguished above all others by its hideousness. Unless we can act as Irishmen we shall become the Japanese of Europe, capable only of imitation.'

There is nothing sadder than the failure of a dream, but few have capsized so totally as the Sinn Féin dream of the 1916 Rebellion. Sinn Féin means 'Ourselves' and implied that, if necessary by blood sacrifice, our Irish cultural identity must be preserved. Now, as I

— *A Visit to Hesse and Some Thoughts about Princes* —

write, seventy-eight Japanese businessmen are in Dublin to teach us how to imitate their imitations and as an earnest of their concern for us have bought a million pound's worth of pork.

Sadly I move from Ireland to Germany, where the Butler Society spent one of its happiest and most successful rallies in August 1968. To me it was deeply interesting, for here was a family society that had gone on for eighty years and still showed no signs of failing, where old families, despite wars and revolution, still live in family homes. I observed how all these German houses seemed to reach out towards posterity with an assurance which we have mostly lost. It is this that gives to the least pretentious of them a dignity combined with domesticity that is becoming everywhere rarer. I believe that the continuity of a country's culture rests with families not with governments and county councils, and that it is Ireland's loss that of all the many hundreds of Butler castles (to mention one historic family alone), all but one are ruins, waiting patiently for the bulldozer.

Could one reason for Anglo-Irish apathy be that great empires act centripetally on their subjects and that the German empire was not old enough to overcome those family and regional loyalties, which keep a national identity alive?

I was in the archives room of several castles and mansions of the von Buttlars of Hesse who claim kinship with the Irish and English Butlers. At Markershausen they have a unique portrait of the fifth Earl of Ormonde, who was beheaded in the Wars of the Roses, and Horst von Buttlar-Brandenfels had made a small museum to illustrate family history, German, English and Irish. In Schloss Elberberg there are trunks full of letters, diaries, records of the part played by the von Buttlars in the Thirty Years' War.

The von Buttlars, a large and once-powerful family, who since the thirteenth century have lived in the wooded hills that border Thuringia and East Germany, have had their regular *Familientag* for several generations and they still keep in touch with members of their family now divided from them by political barriers. One day they took us to Oberkaufungen where we saw the council chamber, church and administrative offices of the Althessische Ritterschaft. When the Landgrave of Hesse still reigned in Kassel, there must have been here a busy centre of authority; thirty of the noble families of Hesse still survive and I believe that, like the von Buttlars, they still have their own *Familientag* and a sense of family solidarity that has long since died out in Ireland and England.

In the church, Vetter Adolf von Buttlar-Stiedenrode laid a wreath on the war memorial in memory of all the Butlers who died on either side in two world wars. The Ritterschaft, though politically powerless, still owns corporately the medieval settlement with its assembly rooms, stables, coach houses and vast surrounding forests of Oberkaufungen. There is a

A Visit to Hesse and Some Thoughts about Princes

well-preserved skeleton here of an organization that was once active and powerful. What was it like in its prime?

Now that everywhere power has passed to oil companies and steel corporations, and that the Volkswagen factory at Kassel could no doubt buy out the Landgrave of Hesse and all his nobility, one can consider objectively the German principalities and their courts. Is there anything at all to be said for small-scale paternalism (a neutral word, for fathers can be bad as well as good)?

Liberal historians would agree with H. A. L. Fisher, who called the German princes 'the idlest and most selfish aristocracy in Europe'. They were powerful, too. When the Landgrave Philip of Hesse espoused Protestantism, all his subjects had to follow suit and, when he divorced his wife, Luther himself was obliged to find in the Bible a justification for polygamy.

A later Landgrave sold Hessian soldiers to the British Government to fight against the American rebels in 1780 and the Irish rebels in 1798. About half of them were killed and he spent the sale-price of three million pounds on science, literature, the arts and the adornment of his capital. I am told that the large Hercules building in Wilhelms Hohe with its maze of fountains and terraces and its *Wasservexierungsportplatz* (you invite your friends into a grotto and put ten pfennigs into a slot machine and they are 'water-vexed' from many little jets in the rock) was paid for by selling tall

Hessians to Frederick the Great, who collected them for a special regiment.

How very wicked! But the arts thrived in Kassel. The Landgraves bought nineteen Rembrandts for the gallery and took pride in those clever citizens who invented the first logarithmic tables, the first theodolite, the first German commercial bank, the first herbarium, steam engine and chime of bells. The brothers Grimm initiated there the science of philology, and their famous fairy tales laid the foundations of folklore. And now when a prosperous city of 200,000 inhabitants has been erected on the ruins left by Hitler's war, it is to the surviving achievements of the Landgraves and their nobility that the sightseer and foreign tourist are almost exclusively directed.

Could one say that, as nurseries of talent and the arts, these tiny states surpassed the great ones that gobbled them up? About this, German genius is divided. Schiller constantly satirized their pompous little courts, but he judged them by his own experiences, which by our standards were not very terrible at all. The Duke of Wurtemberg arrested him because he gave up his medical studies to write plays and left Stuttgart without permission, But he escaped to another duke, got a pension from a third, and ended his life with Goethe and Herder at the court of Weimar.

In Weimar, Karl August the duke had put Goethe in charge of the mines, the roads, the treasury, the university of the little state; he directed its theatre. His life

— *A Visit to Hesse and Some Thoughts about Princes* —

overflowed with rich and varied small-scale experiences, and it was in these years that he wrote his greatest works, made his remarkable discoveries in botany and anatomy, and became a European figure.

There is reason in this. An independent mind is always feared and detested, but the stupider princes were too capricious and jealous of each other to gang up effectively against it. If some gifted rebel like Luther or Schiller fell out with his prince, there were a dozen other rival states in which he could find asylum; he did not, like Einstein or Thomas Mann, have to leave Germany altogether. If censorship is to be effective, a high degree of social co-ordination and a loyal civil service is necessary. These were nineteenth-century achievements and because of them, German genius, which stagnated under Bismarck and Kaiser Wilhelm, was extinguished in the days of *Ein Volk, Ein Reich, Ein Führer*.

The princes were, of course, very ordinary people, operating in a familiar social cycle. Were the petty princes of Italy during the Renaissance very different? Robbers became robber-barons, who became barons, who became victims of robbers, who became . . . Irish history makes the process well known to us. There was in the nineteenth century a delusion that the amalgamation of robber-families into robber-states would arrest the cycle or make it more humane, civilized, creative. The reverse has happened.

In the days when genius flourished in Hesse the most publicized event was when the coopers of Kassel made an enormous barrel upon the surface of the frozen Fulda river and brought it in a gay procession as a present for the Landgrave. Much later, Bismarck, in the process of unifying Germany, deposed the Landgrave and annexed Hesse to Prussia. Everyone, including the Hessians, thought this was progress. Kassel became a vast railway and road junction; then a huge factory for the making of machine tools appeared. The Volkswagen factory and Henschel works followed. Kassel grew and grew till in the late war it became an obvious target for the British Air Force, which by persistent bombing over many weeks destroyed the entire city, old and new.

The huge fires could be seen at Göttingen, fifty miles away, and did worse then expunge the city. They seem to have sterilized the soil in which it was built. Anyone who has made a bonfire in a field knows that for a long time only nettles and thistles will thrive where the grass-roots have been scorched.

The new Cassel, though prosperous, is like any other big modern city. Everything in its shops, its theatres, its cinemas, is mass-produced, derivative. It is a faceless, joyless place. Apart from its German shop-signs, it might be in Kansas or Lancashire. When it attracts another bomb, bigger and better, there will, apart from men and women, be only a vast and smothered spiritual potential to regret. Or is it possible that before then, by the study of the past, some new way of realizing the great and generous German genius will be discovered?

– The Children of Drancy –
[1968/78]

Lately I was comparing three versions of the story of the Children of Drancy and it occurred to me that we mostly have more detailed information, more curiosity, about remote and now irrelevant events like the murder of the two little Princes in the Tower in the summer of 1483 or the death of 123 English people in the Black Hole of Calcutta on 19 June 1756. Two of the writers I consulted said it was in July, a third said it was in August 1942 that the 4,051 children were sent off to be killed in Poland from the transit camp at Drancy north of Paris. Were they French Jews or foreigners? Were they girls or boys? It is usually said boys, but suburban residents on the outskirts of Paris who heard them wailing at night say they were little girls, and there is a story of a bleeding ear torn by a harried police inspector as he removed an earring.

They spent four days without food at the Vélodrome d'Hiver (the winter cycle-racing stadium) before their mothers were taken from them, then they were loaded three or four hundred at a time into cattle trains at the Gare d'Austerlitz and taken to Auschwitz. It was related at Nuremberg that an order came from Berlin that deportees from Vichy France should be mingled discreetly with the children to make them look like family groups. Was this done? It is not as though dubious legend has grown up around these children as it has around King Herod's far smaller enterprise in Bethlehem. The facts are bleak and few. It should not be hard to find more and to iron out discrepancies. But no one seems interested.

I believe we are bored because the scale is so large that the children seem to belong to sociology and statistics. We cannot visualize them reading Babar books, having their teeth straightened, arranging dolls' tea parties. Their sufferings are too great and protracted to be imagined, and the range of human sympathy is narrowly restricted.

Had four or five children only been killed and burnt, and had it happened outside the booking office at the Gare d'Austerlitz, we would have responded emotionally and probably their names and their fate would have been carved on a marble tablet like that which commemorates the victims of the Black Hole outside the Post Office in Calcutta. And the names of their murderers would be remembered for ever. But to kill and burn 4,051 children after transporting them to Poland was a huge co-operative endeavour, in which thousands of French and German policemen, typists, railway officials, gas-fitters and electricians were engaged. It was composite villainy, and when you try to break it down there are no villains, just functionaries as neutral and characterless as the clusters of ink

— *The Children of Drancy* —

blobs of which a press photograph is composed. The officials who handled the children were, we are told, deeply affected. Even the Vichy Commissioner for Jewish Affairs, Louis Darquier, who deported Jews in their thousands from France, had suggested that the children be transferred to a French orphanage, but he did nothing about it. Though Pierre Laval, the French Premier, was enthusiastic about the deportation of all foreign Jews, even those under sixteen, neither he nor Pétain realized that they were not going to be 'settled' in the East but killed there.

Even at the peak of the organizational pyramid one finds duty, routine, idealism of a kind more often than sadism as the motive power; in the interests of a more glorious future the tender impulses had to be suppressed. At the Jerusalem trial even the most hostile witnesses failed to prove that Eichmann, an exemplary husband and father, had ever been guilty of wanton cruelty. These people were really what they claimed to be, idealists, whose seedy ideals would never have germinated and pullulated in any other century but ours.

However confident we may be of the facts, there are irreconcilable divergences when we come to their interpretation. 'Too much science,' say some. 'Too much literary scorn for science,' say others. François Mauriac, who was in Paris at the time, wrote some twenty years later:

— THE INVADER WORE SLIPPERS —

Nothing I had seen during those sombre years of the Occupation had left so deep a mark on me as those trainloads of Jewish children standing at the Gare d'Austerlitz. Yet I did not even see them myself. My wife described them to me, her voice still filled with horror. At that time we knew nothing of Nazi methods of extermination. And who could have imagined them? Yet the way these lambs had been torn from their mothers in itself exceeded anything we had so far thought possible. I believe that on that day I touched upon the mystery of iniquity whose revelation was to mark the end of one era and the beginning of another. The dream which Western man conceived in the eighteenth century, whose dawn he thought he saw in 1789, and which, until 2 August, 1914, had grown stronger with the process of enlightenment and the discoveries of science – this dream vanished finally for me before those trainloads of little children. And yet I was still thousands of miles away from thinking that they were to be fuel for the gas chamber and crematorium.

Yet even at the time few thought like that. It is easier to forget about the Children of Drancy than to liberate ourselves from the increasing control that science has over our lives. The year after Mauriac wrote what I have quoted, Charles Snow delivered at Cambridge his famous lecture on 'The Two Cultures' in which he claimed that the traditional culture of the past, and science, the culture of the future, should make peace with one another. Charles Snow, a novelist himself, addressed his lecture mainly to the 'traditional' man of letters, scolding him for being ignorant of elementary scientific knowledge like molecular biology and the Second Law of Thermodynamics.

He quoted with approval someone he referred to as 'a distinguished scientist':

Why do most writers take on social opinions which would have been thought uncivilized at the time of the Plantagenets? Wasn't that true of most of the famous writers of the twentieth century – Yeats, Pound, Wyndham Lewis – nine out of ten of those who have dominated literary sensitivity in our time? Weren't they not only politically silly, but politically wicked? Didn't the influence of all they represent bring Auschwitz that much nearer?

Snow scolds Ruskin, William Morris, Thoreau, Emerson and D. H. Lawrence for their rebellion against the Age of Science: 'They tried various fancies, which were not in effect more than screams of horror.'

I dislike quoting Snow when he talks nonsense or endorses other people's nonsense (when I was younger I enjoyed his novels and in 1941 wrote a rave review of *The Masters* in *The Bell*). As an Irishman, who knew Yeats, I can only gasp when the great Irish poet is linked with Auschwitz.

Snow's lecture caused tremendous interest. It was published and many times reprinted. There was a three-week long correspondence in *The Spectator,* most of it favourable to Snow. He was thinking on popular lines. When he wrote his novels he was Charles Snow, then he became Sir Charles, and finally Lord Snow.

— THE INVADER WORE SLIPPERS —

Only F. R. Leavis, Professor of English Literature at Cambridge, reacted violently. He delivered and later printed a lecture furiously attacking Snow, denouncing him as few leading writers have been denounced before. He too was printed in *The Spectator* and there was much comment, most of it hostile.

Snow [writes Leavis] takes inertly the characteristic and disastrous confusion of the civilization he is trying to instruct.

He is intellectually as undistinguished as it is possible to be.

He thinks he has literary culture and scientific culture. In fact he has neither.

He rides on an advancing swell of cliché without a glimmer of what creative literature is or what it signifies.

Who will assert that the average member of a modem society is more fully human or alive than an Indian peasant?

As a novelist he doesn't exist. He can't be said to know what a novel is.

Leavis is an ardent champion of D. H. Lawrence, and, possibly, compared to Lawrence, Snow as a novelist is negligible.

Leavis mentions the Indian because Snow had a detailed plan for rescuing the poorer peoples of the world by means of a scientific revolution. He thought, for instance, that the USA and Britain should educate ten or twenty-thousand scientific specialists 'to the level of Part 1 Natural Science or Mechanized Science Tripos' and send them to India, Africa and South-East

— *The Children of Drancy* —

Asia to help industrialize the inhabitants and lever them out of their pre-scientific stagnation.

How could Snow fail to see that the transportation of six million Jews to the camps was, like the atom bomb, among the most sensational of science's achievements and that, in the international field, science is more often used as an instrument of hatred than of neighbourly love. Think of the export of arms to Iran and to the Contras in Nicaragua, and indeed of the great build-up of armaments all over the globe.

He was surely driven to entertain these visions, more fantastic than the dreams of William Morris, by his knowledge that science was in fact irresistible and had enormous potentialities for good and evil, which only the men of traditional culture, if they accepted it and understood it a little, might be able to control. If they know a little about genetics, for example, they might be able to monitor and arrest the appalling experiments of the geneticists, which now only religious leaders with the wisdom and authority of the pre-scientific centuries behind them can forbid. They might have persuaded the Americans to industrialize Vietnam (if the Vietnamese wanted to be industrialized) rather than devastate it. But at present the average man of letters knows nothing of science and most scientists are culturally illiterate. Snow says that the average scientist, when one tries to probe what books he'd read, would modestly confess, 'Well, I've tried a bit of Dickens.' Snow himself must have guessed that the gulf between the Two Cultures is unbridgeable.

Has any decade seen so much sophisticated science-promoted violence as the Eighties? All over the world, in small countries and large ones, men who could not invent a pop-gun themselves have access to the newest and most lethal weapons. In Ireland the IRA get their arms from Libya and pay for them by kidnapping the owners of supermarkets (the ransom is always paid and then lied about). Where do the Libyans get their arms from? Who knows? A brisk trade goes on all round the world and the great powers are helpless to end it.

For Mauriac, the eighteenth-century dream of a future enlightened by the discoveries of science had died at Drancy. In England Aldous Huxley and George Orwell had earlier predicted all sorts of horrors. In his book *The Revolt of the Masses* (1932) the Spaniard Ortega Y. Gasset had analyzed what was happening much more accurately: 'Technicism, in combination with liberal democracy, had engendered the Mass Man . . . Modern science has handed over the command of public life to the intellectually commonplace.' Observe the calibre of the world leaders of 1987.

Snow would have none of this. 'The scientific edifice of the physical world is in its intellectual depth, complexity and articulation the most beautiful and wonderful work of the mind of man.' In fact beauty is in the eye of the beholder. A primrose by the river's brim is just as likely to dazzle it as the structure of the haemoglobin molecule. All nature can be seen as beautiful.

— *The Children of Drancy* —

According to Snow let the Two Cultures but unite and educate those twenty-thousand Mechanical Science Tripos men and the gap between the rich and the poor will be bridged, overpopulation checked and atomic war averted.

Most thinking men stand midway between the despair of Orwell and Mauriac from which only the grace of God can rescue us and the twenty-thousand Tripos men, but believe that God and the Tripos men are slowly converging. Though they might express themselves differently, they would concur with the prayer which Major Cooper, the heroic astronaut, composed on his seventeenth orbit round the earth; it ends:

Help us in future space endeavours to show the world that democracy really can compete and still is able to do things in a big way and is able to do research development and conduct new scientific and technical programmes.

Be with all our families. Give us guidance and encouragement and let them know that everything will be okay. We ask in Thy name. Amen.

Though the joint session of Congress to which this prayer was read approved of it, a Hindu about to be industrialized might complain that life is more complex than Major Cooper and Charles Snow believed. A certain intellectual simplicity is the price that has to be paid for irrigation and tractors and freedom from famine and disease. An idea that has to travel far by modern means and circulate freely among alien people must, like an air passenger's luggage, be very meagre indeed.

In spite of that, most men would sooner believe in the healing powers of scientific research and technology than accept François Mauriac's counsel of despair.

But the true answer of the scientific optimist to Mauriac will not, I think, be found by Major Cooper in outer space or by those twenty-thousand Tripos men. Should one not consider the question of size and whether we really have 'to do things in a big way'?

Anti-Semitism, the idea which killed the Children of Drancy, was small and old and had existed for centuries in small pockets all over Europe. If humane ideals had been cultivated as assiduously as technical ones it would long ago have died without issue in some Lithuanian village. But science gave it wings and swept it by aeroplane and wireless and octuple rotary machines all over Europe and even lodged it in Paris, the cultural capital.

No one likes thinking on these lines. Yet observe how even pity can become helpless and sometimes destructive when it is divorced from deep personal concern and becomes a public matter. Public pity forms committees, sends tinned meat, secures entry visas, but the beating of its collective heart can be heard from miles away and it is easily eluded. Those in charge of the children eluded it by taking them to Auschwitz. It was to dodge public pity that the children were

— *The Children of Drancy* —

torn from their mothers and travelled alone or with doomed strangers. The mothers, when their future first became known, preferring death for their children to the lonely fate they foresaw for them, had started to throw them down from the tops of buildings. They would have continued to do this from the railway carriage windows and the dead or dying bodies might have roused some dormant committee into action in France or Germany or Poland.

Something similar was happening in Free Europe. As the funds of the refugee committees swelled, the price of liberty for a Jew went higher and higher. The compassion of the Allies, turned into cash, could be used against them. In 1944 Allied pity could have saved a million Jews in return for 100,000 trucks, but the trucks would have been used against Russia and so divided the Allies and resuscitated the latent anti-Semitism of the Russians. Looking at the matter in the large way it was better even for Jewry as a whole that a further million Jews should die.

Because of these complexities the Children of Drancy will always remain shadowy figures, and as nursery symbols of the vast cruelty of the world we shall go on using Herod and the little princes and the Black Hole. These stories are educative because they are about wicked men who can be punished or at least reviled, and not about that Faceless and Mysterious Collective Iniquity against which we are powerless. It is not a satisfactory choice, all the same, because historians now think that Herod never massacred the Innocents and that Richard Crookback never smothered the princes and that Suraja Dowlah thought the Black Hole was properly ventilated, whereas no one denies what happened to the Children of Drancy.

It is because we do things in the big way that the Wicked Man has now become so elusive and almost an abstraction. The chain of responsibility lengthens every day; we can think of it as an immense row of Part 1 Science Tripos graduates holding hands across the earth and linking together the triumphs of civilization to a depth of savage misery which the Aztecs, because they never discovered the wheel, could not inflict upon their victims. Snow mentions with approval a prototype of these Tripos men, a Prussian called Siemens, a pioneer in electrical engineering over a hundred years ago. I prepared this paper by the light of electricity that was brought from the great dam at Ardnacrusha on the river Shannon by Messrs Siemens a generation ago; each bulb had 'Siemens, made in Germany' printed on it. In this way Siemens helped to modernize Ireland, but Ireland was only one link in a long chain. In November 1932 Karl von Siemens used his wealth and influence to bring Hitler to power and later his firm installed the electricity at Auschwitz, where of course it was not used just for reading lamps and making toast. There too, as at Lublin, Siemens set up factories for the employment of slave labour, while for their factory at Berlin Haselhaorst they bought seven hundred wom-

— *The Children of Drancy* —

en from the SS at Ravensbruck at four to six marks a head. The directors of Siemens were on the American list of German industrialists to be prosecuted at Nuremberg, but probably they were all humane and agreeable men belonging to the upper, beneficent end of the long chain; anyway, the charges against them were dropped. On the other hand, Ezra Pound, who had, on his own responsibility and not as a link in a chain, given much foolish praise to the Fascists, was punished and arraigned. Yet he had never killed or enslaved anybody.

It will always be so. A mischievous poet is like a thorn in the finger. He can be pulled out. But the mischief that results from a concentration of Tripos men is like disseminated sclerosis. And that is another reason why we talk so little about the Children of Drancy.

Charles Snow was surely right when he said that most literary intellectuals are 'natural Luddites'. I think he meant that they continue to worry when worry is useless. Ruskin, Morris, Thoreau, Lawrence, all repudiated the new world to which engineer Siemens was devoting his genius, but even a century ago it was hard already to contract out while now it is all but impossible. Should I read by candlelight because the firm that gave me electricity illuminated also the last agony of the Children of Drancy? I don't think so. I am less frightened of science than I am of that doctrine of the Mystery of Iniquity, which is to many the only consolation left now that there is no traffic on the road to Brook Farm, and New

Harmony is sealed off. The Mystery of Iniquity has its roots in despair, but wickedness would no longer be mysterious if the chains of responsibility were shorter and science, which lengthened those chains, must be forced to go into reverse and shorten them.

Fortunately there are still small communities where the Wicked Man is not yet woven so scientifically into the fabric of society that he cannot be extracted without stopping the trains and fusing the electric light. It is not a coincidence that two small countries, Denmark and Bulgaria, stemmed the flow to Auschwitz better than any of their more powerful neighbours on the continent. Apart from size the two countries have nothing in common. The Bulgars are primitive, the Danes a highly sophisticated people. They are no doubt individually as wicked as the rest of us, but wickedness still has a name and an address and a face. When the rumour, a false one, went round Sofia that the government intended to deport its Jews, the citizens demonstrated outside the Palace and blocked the roads to the railway station. In Denmark on the night of 1 October 1943, when the Jews heard they were to be rounded up, each family knew which Danish family was prepared to hide them. Very few were caught. At the Gare d'Austerlitz the Children of Drancy were surrounded by the most civilized and humane people in Europe, but they were scarcely less isolated and abandoned than when they queued up naked for their 'shower-bath' in the Polish forest.

— *The Children of Drancy* —

But I must answer the charge made by Snow's scientist that W. B. Yeats 'brought Auschwitz nearer', because by focussing his mind on distant horizons Snow failed to see what was under his nose. Yeats deliberately chose the small community, moving his heart and his body and as much as he could of his mind from London to Ireland, his birthplace. For him and a dozen other well-known Irish writers Ireland had been a larger Brook Farm, a refuge whose walls were built not by some transcendental theory but by history and geography. For a few years our most parochial period became also our most creative. If there was in Yeats a Fascist streak it derived from his disillusionment with the drab unheroic Ireland in which the dreams of the visionaries of 1916 had ended. He complained that 'men of letters lived like outlaws in their own country'. When he saw that Irish Fascism promised to be as drab and demagogic as Irish democracy, he rapidly back-pedalled and rewrote the song he had composed for the Blue Shirts, making it so fantastic that no political party could sing it. He led the campaign against the Irish censorship and in everything he did and said he was a champion of intellectual and moral and social freedom.

In all this he was an isolated figure and even in Ireland the range of his influence was very small. But in my opinion personal and parochial efforts like his did form a real obstruction on the road to Auschwitz, whereas its traffic was never once interrupted by conventional weapons.

The courage of the astronauts, the talents of the twenty-thousand Tripos men are needed, but they must break down, link by link, those long chains of atomized guilt with which the Children of Drancy were strangled.

POSTSCRIPT

The Children of Drancy were not totally forgotten in France. On 5 November 1978 a programme on the last days of Marshal Pétain was to be screened. It was abruptly withdrawn and a film on the Renaissance Pope Clement VII was substituted. The reason was that there had been a remarkable national re-examination of conscience in France due to an interview published in *L'Express* with the eighty-year-old Darquier, the Vichy Government's Commissioner for Jewish Affairs, whom I have mentioned already. Despite the kindly intentions towards the Children of Drancy with which he has been credited, he had deported 75,721 French Jews to German concentration camps, including the Children. He was so virulent an anti-Semite that even the Germans were surprised by his zeal. He escaped to Spain and was condemned to death in his absence but this was soon forgotten. After a pause he changed his name to d'Arquier de Pellepoix and, an elegant figure with a monocle, he became a welcome guest in the cocktail circles of Franco's Spain. It was here that the enterprising correspondent of *L'Express* contacted

— *The Children of Drancy* —

him thirty-three years after the war was over. He was a sick man crippled by hardening of the arteries, but he still enjoyed the protection of many leading figures, military and political, and he met the correspondent's enquiries with amused condescension. The six million concentration camp deaths, he declared, were a Jewish invention. 'They were all of them exported to new homes in Central Europe,' he said. 'The only victims of the Auschwitz gas-ovens', he added, 'were fleas.' (I suppose he meant that their clothes were fumigated in preparation for their new life.) He refused to look at the photographs of the piles of gas-chamber victims. 'Jewish fakes!' he exclaimed.

The whole of France was moved by the new revelations. President Giscard d'Estaing and Prime Minister Barre warned about the treatment of their Nazi past on the television screen and the press. Simone Veil, the Minister of Health, was profoundly stirred. She had been deported to Auschwitz with her family at the age of fourteen.

'It is the first time since the war,' she said in the National Assembly, 'that anyone has dared to go so far.' There were pictures of Auschwitz and the other death camps shown on television and in the press. There was a clamour to have Darquier extradited. There was much indignation that French television refused to acquire the American series 'Holocaust'. 'Too expensive,' one network said, and an artist Marek Halter opened a fund for private donations to contribute to the cost.

Then the public prosecutor, acting on orders from the Minister of Justice, opened a new case against Darquier for 'defence of war-crimes and incitement to racial hatred'. But Spain has never extradited political offenders to France and time had run out under the twenty-year Statute of Limitations.

– Peter's Window –
[1984]

No. 59 Chernishev Pereulok was a large plum-coloured block of bourgeois flats near the Yekaterinsky Sad (the Catharine Gardens), and the Archangelskys' flat was on the fifth floor. The lift had not worked since 1917 and sat in the well of the staircase, full of tram tickets and old newspapers. There was still a large gilt mirror on their landing, though all the others had been removed by the Jacht or House Committee. Darya Andreyevna, the former owner of the flat and its 'responsible tenant', set great store by all these traces of former grandeur and the Jacht had yielded before her fury when the mirror was threatened.

When my wife, Peggy, and I and our friend Archie Lyall first came to Leningrad in 1931 on the *Alexei Rykov,* a tourist ship, the Archangelskys had made a special effort to welcome us. We brought news of Nikolai Mihalitch's old friends in England with whom he had had no contact since his wife, Connie, and baby son had left. They had gone home three years ago when the NEP period had given place to the rigours of the Five Year Plan and milk and baby-foods became scarce. We got the introduction to Nikolai Mihalitch through my cousin, Willy de Burgh, Professor of Philosophy at

Reading University. Nikolai's father had been a priest in Tiflis and they had fled from the Bolsheviks to the Crimea (for a short time in White Russian hands). There, his sister had married an Englishman, an officer in the British interventionist forces, whose home was in Reading. When the Bolsheviks seized the Crimea, Nikolai was sent to England and became one of the most brilliant of de Burgh's pupils. It was there that, later, he married Connie, a fellow student, and influenced by the left-wing intellectualism of the time, they became Communists and decided to join his widowed mother in Leningrad.

When we first called there were biscuits and tea with hot milk, and strawberry jam in saucers, and his mother was in a state of collapse compounded of hospitality and suspicion. Nikolai had asked a friend of his, Major Tihomirov, a teacher in the Military Academy, to meet us and a colleague of his own, Baroness Garatinsky, was anxiously awaited. Nikolai Mihalitch had told me her story. She had been an old revolutionary and in 1917 her peasants, who had taken over her estates in Central Russia, had made her their manager. Five years later her position had became impossible and she was now teaching languages in Leningrad. Through the open window we saw her limping slowly up the street, pausing and glancing up and down to see that it was empty before she turned in. 'It isn't very safe for us to visit each other,' he said; 'in any case she doesn't like the stairs with her lame leg, but this is a

— *Peter's Window* —

special occasion.' He told me that because of her origins, she was suspect politically. She had a daughter in exile in Siberia and a son in Solovietski Island. In Goskurs, the Polytechnic where she taught, she was the victim of petty persecution. 'Women are the worst,' he said, and he was explaining how in Leningrad an arts education was more accessible to the female than to the male bourgeois, when the baroness walked in. She paused in the doorway, leaning on her stick, and diverted with a smile his mother's effort to introduce us and give her a chair. 'Later, later, Nina Gavrilovna.' To us she said, 'Women are allowed a bit more licence, because even here they aren't taken seriously. Masculine unreliability matters more.'

She had a sharp rather cantankerous manner but spoke English well in a beautifully clear voice. She always talked rapidly and provocatively when she was manoeuvring into chairs or difficult positions, as if to distract attention. She looked coldly into people's eyes when she talked to them. She herself had a lack of personal inquisitiveness that was almost unfriendly. It was as if she could only argue or disagree and did not waste time in liking or disliking.

Nina Gavrilovna was a crushed, dark little woman. She followed our English talk anxiously with her bright black eyes, interrupting her son with nudges and murmurs, when she could: 'Kolya, ask the lady after the Professor's wife's health!' 'Kolya, you are talking so much you have not noticed the lady has nothing on her plate!' (Only Nikolai's mother called him Kolya, as I will for brevity, but actually everybody in the flat was very formal and used patronymics. Even his closest friends called him Nikolai Mihalitch.)

She guessed correctly that her son was being indiscreet but could never learn that it made him worse to interrupt. The baroness, seeing her agitation, said to me, 'You mustn't think that because we have much to complain of, we are enemies of the Revolution. The Revolution had to happen, it was the result of generations of suffering and plotting. All the great Russians of the past have played a part in it. It is a historical fact, a great convulsion of human nature. If we are to go on living we must accept it, and I have always done so gladly.'

Before we could reply Tihomirov succeeded in changing the conversation. He spoke English in the genteel, mincing way of some educated Russians. He had gold teeth and a moist, glinting smile.

As we left, Kolya said to me, 'When you come back from Rostov, you must stay with me. I will get you a job teaching.' He translated this to his mother, who gave a glance of agony. 'But there is no bed. What will Darya Andreyevna say?' He ignored her. 'I will arrange. I will get you a bed. You must stay a term.'

We went down the Volga and visited Moscow and Rostov. Archie Lyall wrote a book on our experiences, *Russian Roundabout,* which became a classic for all earlier travellers by Intourist. I came back fearing that

Kolya's mother would have dissuaded him from inviting me to stay on. I was wrong. We spent a few days in Leningrad before the *Rykov* sailed back and it was plain Kolya counted on my staying. Smiling and bowing, Alexander Ivanitch Tihomirov came to our hotel and together we went to the military stores, where, under his guidance, I bought myself a camp-bed for forty roubles. The next day the *Rykov* sailed. Kolya, Tihomirov and I went to the docks to see off Peggy and Archie. It was a strange departure, for there was a young woman among the passengers who had had a nervous breakdown. She had been recommended a 'complete change' and she and her parents could think of nothing better than a trip to Russia. While there she had gone mad and had to be dragged aboard kicking and struggling and finally lifted up the gangway, screaming.

That afternoon I installed myself in Chernishev Pereulok. It was the name-day of all the Sonias and Nadezhdas, and their friends were hurrying up and down the streets carrying bunches of overblown dahlias. A few foreigners were still bathing on the broad strand by the Peter and Paul fortress but the melon pips, which had started to sprout by the water's rim, had been nipped by an early frost. Workmen were wrapping up the heads of delicate shrubs in the Summer Garden in balloons of paper and taking in the cactuses and coleuses, which ornamented the lawns with hammers and sickles.

— THE INVADER WORE SLIPPERS —

In the Archangelskys' flat the Jacht had sent a chimney sweep to clean the flue. Everything I saw was coloured and penetrated for me by the thought of the Revolution. Even commonplace or inevitable things had a bloom of special significance because they had matured at such a time and in such a place.

I pitched my camp-bed between the stove and the window in the room, where we had our tea-party in the summer. Kolya had a divan covered with drab fusty material in the opposite corner. Everthing in the room was shabby and dark. There were large patches on the wall where his son, Misha, a couple of years before had peeled off the wallpaper and scribbled on the plaster. Over the whole flat there was that sweetish, musty smell of black bread and benzine and scent and galoshes that Russians seem to carry with them, even into exile. I felt lonely and ill-at-ease. Nina Gavrilovna plainly did not want me there. She refused to believe that being foreign I could understand anything, unless she shouted at me with plentiful gesticulations. Her bed was in a widening of the passage, which was screened off by a dark curtain. Beyond that were two rooms, where invisible factory-workers lived. To the left was the room of Darya Andreyevna and her husband. In the dark passage outside our room near the front door, Lyubotchka, the Archangelskys' maid, used to sleep on her trunk. Till I had practice I stumbled over her every time I came to bed late. At the far end of the passage was the kitchen, where each tenant had his private Primus, and off that

— *Peter's Window* —

there were two windowless cupboards, the bathroom and the W.C. Darya had asserted her authority in these two rooms by pinning up the pictures that decorated the flat when it had been hers, 'Stags at Bay', 'The Imperial Palace at Gatchina', family groups. They bulged out from their drawing-pins with all the fluff and dust that had accumulated behind them. No one dared to remove them, but during the paper shortage hard-pressed tenants had torn jagged strips from them and from their cardboard mounts.

Kolya had exchanged his Russian white summer suit for a Norfolk jacket and grey flannel trousers. Before he was like an Italian but now he was like a Bloomsbury Asiatic. He had a dark thin fanatical face and abrupt, vehement movements. He did not like to explain or to have his explanations questioned.

My first day I spent alone in the flat writing letters and examining Kolya's books. They were neatly shelved on a pair of skis that he was storing for his elder brother, an engineer. I saw F. H. Bradley, Hegel, Bertrand Russell, Aldous Huxley, D. H. Lawrence. Of Russian writers he had only Lenin and his commentators.

I was interrupted constantly by the telephone. His mother would slip in and answer it, looking at me through the corners of her eyes. 'Ne doma,' she would say bitterly, 'Ne znaioo!' 'He's not at home.' 'I don't know!' This happened two or three times. Then she took out her basket and went marketing, and I was left to answer the next call myself three-quarters of an hour later. It was a lady. 'Where is Nikolai Mihalitch?' From my way of answering she guessed I was English and she went on in English. 'Where can he be? He was due to give his lesson here half an hour ago and I rang up Techmass, but he hadn't given his class there, and at Goskurs it was the same.' I couldn't enlighten her.

At six o'clock his mother let him in and there was a voluble conversation in the passage. He came into the room without greeting me. He looked completely exhausted. 'It is arranged,' he said, but hearing his mother at the door leapt up and seized a plate of overcooked vegetable marrow from her. 'Isn't your mother going to eat here?' I asked. 'No, it would be better not. She does not understand the English.' Even when it was irrelevant, I made a point of saying I was Irish not English. I made things worse by saying once that the de Burghs were Irish too. It was as a visitor from England, where he had been so happy, that Kolya was welcoming me. For years he had been waiting for an opportunity to return the kindness which had been shown him. Even for his mother the syllables Dee Buggs had some mystic significance. He did not want to be put off by details.

'What is arranged?' I asked, when he seemed ready for a question. 'Your classes are arranged,' he said. 'You will have four classes every evening from eight till midnight. I've made out the list. You will be a member of our brigade. Then there is Olga Kulgachev two hours and Engineer Stavrogin three hours in a decade, and you've already fixed up with Alexander Ivanitch. They will start next week.' A decade, which sounded to me an eternity, meant ten days. Brigades were groups of friends, who shared out pupils or jobs between each other. There were other brigades for house decoration, theatre craft, translating and all the more specialized arts and crafts. 'But did you spend all this time looking for work for me? You must have missed all your classes.'

'That is of no importance.'

For the next few days he once more gave up all his classes in spite of my protests, and we tramped and trammed from one end of Leningrad to the other, interviewing passport officials, professors, pupils.

One day as we were queuing up outside the offices of the Lensoviet, he tried to explain himself to me: 'I am a Caucasian from Georgia like Stalin, with the same theological background. He was a theological student. He believes like the Manicheans that there is Good and Evil, Black and White, a dichotomy. All this which he thinks Good is Evil.' He waved his hand at the Lensoviet and the long queue.

'Why do you like the English so much then? They are not Manichean. They play down all the major issues of good and evil. They are loyal to small obligations, not big ones. I can't imagine an English teacher neglecting all his classes to help the friend of friends, who were once very good to him.'

He looked hurt, as if I had accused him of being

un-English. But I had meant it as a compliment and I could not let the subject drop. I argued that social organization works better in England, simply because the English only made superficial impact on each other. They glide about, cannoning off each other like billiard balls. They can calculate each other's reactions accurately, because they hardly ever impinge. Perhaps the reason why the Russians are difficult to organize is because they make real contact. It's like playing billiards with bull's eyes.

'You forget I am a Caucasian. That's what I hate about the Russians, always prying and enquiring about each other.'

I found his claim to be Caucasian as irritating as he found my claim to be Irish: 'I don't think Russians could ever be detached in the tepid, unemphatic English way. You would merely isolate yourselves.'

After a pause, he said: 'Darya Andreyevna was catechizing my mother about you today. She thinks you are a spy and wants the House Committee to turn you out. She has been to the Upravdom [the President of the House Committee]. Lyubotchka did her best for you. She said she thought you were a harmless idiot because you smile when you talk to her.'

'I only meant to be friendly.'

'Yes, but real Russians only smile at jokes.'

I had no way of paying for my lodgings, so I suggested that Peggy should pay Connie in Eastbourne every week. He refused indignantly. I was his guest. I accepted this but asked Peggy to send suitable things to Connie instead.

But we were to have other complications that evening. Lyubotchka the maid came from Karelia near Finland where not much was known about plumbing. She had broken one of Connie's wedding-present tea cups, and, fearing to admit it, had thrown it down the W.C. and pulled the plug. Darya Andreyevna a little later found the W.C. choked and, groping with her hand, she discovered a piece of Connie's china. With me there without her permission, it was too much for her. Sobbing with rage, she burst through the door and flung the horrible handful on the floor.

In the fury about the tea cup my problem was forgotten. Nobody ever again thought I was a spy. But after that, Darya and Kolya never went to see each other. They communicated, when they had to, by telephone. When our door was open, we could hear Darya Andreyevna's real voice through the passage wall almost as clearly as her telephone voice. Though she lived in the next room for many months, I never saw her again, nor did I ever see her husband though we were incessantly aware of each other.

Darya's husband had been a colonel in the Tsar's army, a very tyrannical one, Kolya told me, and his wife had been an opera singer and quite famous. After the revolution she had sung Soviet songs and had been awarded the rank of 'Naoochnaya Rabotnitsa' or 'Scientific Worker'. Because of this she had first-category food rations and the right to a certain floor space in her old flat. In relation to the Jacht she became 'the responsible tenant'. With her food tickets she could get, among other things, macaroni. Nina Gavrilovna could never forgive her this. A Tsarist colonel's wife got macaroni, while her son, a Marxist professor and Privat Dozent at the Oriental Institute, had to live on vegetable marrow. Incessantly nagging Kolya about this, she had made it psychologically impossible for him ever to get a first-category food ticket. All that was necessary was for him to fill in a few forms, but nothing would induce him to do so. Whenever macaroni was mentioned, his face went dead and cold and Manichean.

Soon after this my classes began. The last tourists had disappeared from the streets and I felt like a privileged member of the audience who goes home with the actors after the play. Stacks of logs were being piled in the courtyards and back streets and one heard the whine of saws. The streets got emptier and footsteps echoed. Everyone except Kolya sealed up his double windows with gummed paper and closed the phortochka, the little ventilating window by which they were pierced. Everyone bought galoshes, for the pavements were like troughs and held water.

I had no winter clothes and clothing became an obsession, for my arms were too long for everything I could afford. Kolya lent me an old coat, and I wedged a pair of undersize galoshes onto my shoes. I could never get them off again, so I used to take off shoes and all at my classes and hide my feet under the desk. Later on I put my galoshes on my indoor shoes, but I had to walk sedately or the galoshes dragged them off again.

One day, as I was walking to my classes in the twilight, I saw a large leather-coated figure lying on the pavement. He had an open dispatch-case beside him with papers scattered about. He was snoring. A woman came from the far side of the Moika river to help me lift him up. 'What a shame,' she exclaimed, 'to see such a beautiful coat lying in the mud!' We examined it together. 'I bet he's a commissar!' she said. 'One can only get a coat like that with valuta.' We dragged him to the Mariinski Theatre and propped him up, sitting against one of the columns of the portico. I told her I had valuta and needed a coat, so she took a pencil and piece of paper out of his dispatch-case and wrote the name of the place where I could get one like it.

Next day I went there. There was only one possible coat but it was still too short in the sleeves. Nina Gavrilovna did not seem to like my wearing Kolya's coat, so I went back several times but could not make up my mind to spend so much money on a coat that did not fit.

Kolya had brought back from England an obsession about fresh air, and was proud that he was the only man among his acquaintances who kept his phortochka open day and night. Alexander Ivanitch Tihomirov told me that Max Müller had once come to

Petersburg to lecturer on Fresh Air but had to postpone his lecture because he had lost his voice. My experience was the same. I always woke up with a sore throat, but it was a point of honour with Kolya not to close the phortochka.

Kolya had two other friends who taught English, besides Tihomirov and Vera Garatinsky. Both of them, Yegunov and Lihachev, came of wealthy families, who had governesses. Yegunov had had a Scottish-governess, whose Glasgow accents reproduced themselves in all his pupils. Lihachev was in the navy and only settled in Leningrad during the winter, when he taught at the Marine Academy. His English was the strangest and the most fluent. Onto a precise bookish English he had grafted a cosmopolitan sailor's slang derived from conversations in the *lingua franca* at Baltic ports. He was never at a loss for a word. We only got two roubles an hour for our classes and big deductions were made for holidays. There were also 'voluntary' contributions, which were compulsory; only Kolya did not pay them, as he disapproved on principle.

Alexander Ivanitch, in those days, was a bachelor with close-cropped hair and a smart military appearance. He had been a Tsarist officer. He was courtly and considerate. He described himself to my wife as 'very Victorian'. But when he deplored the new ways, he did not mean Bolshevism, but foxtrots, red fingernails, James Joyce. The Revolution had been such an overwhelming experience that I doubt if he ever

— *Peter's Window* —

criticized it, even to himself. All the same, to save his self-respect, he permitted himself some tiny heresies, about women in public life, for example. In most totalitarian creeds there is an unimportant corner, like a game-reserve, retained for harmless scepticism and good-humoured satire. Alexander Ivanitch knew his way about it perfectly and for some time appeared to me to be a highly emancipated person.

He had learnt English by the 'Williamson Method' and used to compare his face in a looking-glass with a series of enlarged coloured pictures of the mouth and tongue. He was very conscientious and wished to capture the spirit of the language as well as the idiom. In addition to the mouth-pictures he had a collection of English political speeches on gramophone records. Also he recited to me once a week a leader from *The Manchester Guardian*, which as an officer in the army he was permitted to take in.

He had other military privileges regarding rations of food and clothing, which he shared generously with his friends and the two devoted old ladies who looked after him. He lived in a stuffy room above a tailor's shop. It smelt of pot plants and leather and kvass. He used to put on a record just before my lesson, so as to get his ear into training. One unseasonably warm afternoon I walked with Lihachev towards his house. The loudspeakers on the street corners, which bawled out the feats of shock workers, were silent as if exhausted by the heat, and I was astounded to hear a cultured and fruity English voice echoing unchallenged through the narrow empty street. The voice came from Alexander Ivanitch's open window; it was Mr Asquith addressing a meeting in Edinburgh seventeen years before: 'We shall not sheathe the sword,' he was declaiming, 'till Belgium has recovered in full measure all and more than all that she has lost, till France . . .'

'It is rare and pleasant,' said Lihachev, 'to hear someone praise liberty who has dined well.'

Alexander Ivanitch was revising a pre-revolutionary grammar of English conversation. The questions of the new Russian tourist, instead of being inquisitive and pleasure-seeking, became didactic and uncompromising. He enquired about wages and factories instead of theatres and laundries. The rigours of his catechism were tempered by a strange jauntiness, in which Alexander Ivanitch took a special pride. 'Is a sportlike way of asking the time to say "What do you make the time?"', he enquired, 'and can one use the phrase "oneish twoish" without a preposition?'

I gave him his lessons under seal of secrecy, lest it should get about among rival teachers that he still had anything to learn. Slavs are too logical to value modesty or self-depreciation. 'If you yourself', they argue, 'think poorly of your faculties, they must be poor indeed.'

One day he told me to be very careful what I said to Nikolai Mihalitch. He was unreliable, he explained, and indiscreet. I did not mention that Kolya had given

— *Peter's Window* —

me similar warnings about him. I gathered that Alexander Ivanitch was in touch with the GPU (the Gaypayoo was the current name in 1931 for the Secret Police). In the end I came to the conclusion that almost all those whom I was able to see constantly had obtained the consent of the GPU and were under obligation to report my movements. I was flattered that they liked my company enough to go to this trouble, but I am sure that Alexander Ivanitch alone attempted a conscientious record of my unmemorable sayings and doings.

He was, in fact, the ideal spy. It was a disinterested pleasure to him to gossip, and it was a bonus for him to feel patriotic. He never did us any harm. Indeed, hovering on the edge of our little group, he was a kind of insurance that we should not be molested. He liked his lessons and wished us well. He once publicly refuted a rival teacher's allegation that I had 'a terrible Irish accent'.

Kolya had made out the curriculum for English literature in Techmass and Goskurs. It was very impressive. Every English writer who had written anything vaguely subversive was included. There were Kingsley's *Alton Locke*, Mrs Gaskell's *Mary Barton*, Charlotte Bronte's *Shirley*. Were these about the industrial revolution perhaps? But why Virginia Woolf, Aldous Huxley and E. M. Forster? Copies of the list were typed and I handed them round to my classes and asked them to bring what books they could. About twelve books

THE INVADER WORE SLIPPERS

came: some Byrons, Wildes, Galsworthys, and a book, author unknown, called *A Fairy Sits Upon My Knee*. A little Jewess, who, I had been told, was a political spy, brought in and insisted on reading a book by Mildred Cram about a man who married above himself in London society and did not know that you had to eat asparagus with your fingers. His wife tried to stifle the artistic side of his nature and eventually he flung it all up and returned to his old simple life. No other books could be found. As a result, most classes had to be improvised, and though my pupils were friendly and interested, there was no interval between the four classes, so by midnight I was often nearly speechless from exhaustion.

That winter the fortieth anniversary of Gorki's 'creative work' was being celebrated. Nizhni Novgorod was being rechristened Gorki, and a bombing aeroplane had been dedicated to him. Though we never talked of politics, we sometimes discussed 'ideology'. A woman said that Gorki was 'a gumanist' (our 'h' is 'g' in Russian) and that a bombing aeroplane would not please him much. I asked them to define 'gumanism'. A man said in English, 'It is what you say "namby-pamby".' The woman was not satisfied and began to protest. It appeared that about half the class thought nambi-pambiness a good thing, but the political spy, a kind woman, who did not want trouble, proposed we go on with Mildred Cram.

The classes were orderly and well arranged, the

— *Peter's Window* —

rooms clean and airy. The Principal of Goskurs had once been Director of the Imperial Ballet and all his staff except two or three were bourgeois, who had learnt foreign languages from governesses and tutors. At the doorway sat the political director, an Armenian called Guzelimian. Every time I passed he examined me fiercely, as if he wished to catechize me; he had a villainous peasant face and I hurried on pretending not to notice him. One day when we were alone in the hall he beckoned me over. 'When you go to England,' he said, 'will you get me a fishing-rod?' Fumbling with his papers, he took out a picture. 'Like that. I wanted to talk to you several times, but you looked so stiff I didn't dare.'

The other teachers didn't talk to me but I felt an atmosphere of friendliness and goodwill. Once, when a long corridor was empty, an elderly man, who had never spoken to me, came up and presented me with a book. 'This is my book,' he said. 'Don't tell anyone.' He bolted before I had time to thank him. Whenever I passed him later, he pretended not to see me.

The small blue volume was an excellent Russian-English dictionary by C. K. Bojanus and V. K. Muller. Later Kolya told me that he was Professor Bojanus himself, that he intended to marry Mrs Williamson of the mouth-pictures and go with her to England, but did not want to prejudice his chances of leaving Russia by any association with foreigners.

Edmund Wilson (*New Yorker*, 20 April 1963)

wrote that Bojanus was liquidated and his name taken off the title page of the dictionary, but the verb 'sostavili', 'composed', was left in the plural, though Muller is named as sole author. I had previously heard that he escaped and worked at the School of Slavonic Studies till he died. I reproach myself that I never enquired about this kind, good man, or sent the fishing-rod to Guzelimian.

Nina Gavrilovna was against me from the start and decided that I was to blame for anything that went wrong in the flat. In Moscow I had been given a sixteenth-century ikon of John the Baptist by Leonid Leonov, whose book *The Thief* I had translated, and one day I showed it to Kolya, who promptly hung it on the wall. His mother, seeing it when Kolya was out, was appalled. 'What will his pupils say? It's pearls before swine.' She laid the ikon reverently in the laundry-basket. When Kolya came back and saw the gap on the wall he marched unerringly to the laundry-basket. The ikon came in and out of the basket several times. Then I said to Kolya, 'I'm a nuisance here. I'd better find a room elsewhere.'

He flared up, 'Are you not comfortable here? No one would have you except me; they would be frightened even if they had room. And at the hotel you would have to pay two pounds a day. My mother will be going to Luga soon. At the New Year I will arrange that we take a few days' holiday and go on an excursion with

Lihachev and Yegunov to the South. I will arrange to get teachers' tickets.'

All the same I put several advertisements in the papers and got some replies. I went round to the addresses. Nobody wanted to be paid. In fact money meant very little in Leningrad; they lost all interest in me when they heard I was not a foreign engineer, paid in valuta, and entitled to meal tickets at Quisisana, the Insnab restaurant (Insnab meant Inostranni Snabzheniye or Foreign Provision). One woman thought that as a foreign engineer I would be able to get her coat lined at Torgsin. One letter I did not answer. It was from a Pole called Vaishlé, who offered me a bed in his living-room. His aunt used it in the daytime, but she worked in the post office at night. It would be empty then and I could use it free, if I would help him read an English book on geology. One day when I came back from giving Alexander Ivanitch his lesson, I found Kolya entertaining the Pole, a small fat jolly man. He had brought his lunch and his geology book under his arm. 'I thought you might be too shy to come, so I came instead.' I was relieved to find that in the last resort there was someone in Leningrad eager to house me, and I offered to read some geology with him then and there. As he left, he said, 'I'm in this neighbourhood once or twice a week. I'll just call round and we'll read a bit of geology and I'll promise to keep my aunt's bed free for you.'

I agreed to this arrangement as a sort of retaining fee, and every now and then he came round. He always brought his lunch, but sometimes he came without his geology book just for a talk. Being a Pole, he was the first person I met willing to admit that I was an Irishman. He was greatly interested and told me that Daniel O'Connell's great granddaughter was working in a large china factory on the Neva. He seemed to take it for granted at his first glance at my surroundings that for an Irishman to live in a Russian family was a chemical experiment that might or might not succeed. 'How are things going?' he would ask. 'Remember my aunt's bed is always free.' Once, as he left, he clasped my hand and said: 'You know Russians are Asiatics, they don't understand comfort. I advise you to come to us.'

I had some £25 worth of black roubles, given me by an English sociologist who was staying at the British Embassy. He was going home and no longer needed them. So often I would ask Kolya out to lunch at one of the tourist hotels. After the season the fare was always the same. We had only one course. At the Europa there was a rich-looking pate made of game in aspic, at the October a fish called 'sudak' with Sauce Tartare. Except for ourselves and one waiter, the large dining-rooms were usually empty. The restaurant at the October was below street level and beggars would crouch on the road outside and, stretch in supplicating hands through the ventilators. Kolya came reluctantly or else refused. He was very proud. When I pressed him into coming, in order to show that he had not refused from fear of being compromised, he would talk loudly in English criticizing the Soviet regime. I think he was flattered when one day an old woman came up to us outside the October and said: 'Messieurs, votre roi est le cousin de notre empereur.' He gave her a few kopecks. The old woman looked at them for a moment in hurt perplexity and then stuffed them quickly in her skirt.

In the end I believe it was the Pole and not hunger that prevailed upon Kolya to apply for a first-category food ticket. Though I was the cause of so much trouble, he wanted me to stay. He said one evening: 'I am becoming a "naoochny rabotnik". I have arranged that tomorrow there will be a proper English breakfast. There will be porridge and scrambled eggs.' And next morning Lyubotchka produced a thin custardy substance and 'grechnevaya kasha', a sort of gruel made of buckwheat. The buckwheat only lasted a week, for, learning that Kolya was a naoochny rabotnik, Nadya, one of the Kolya's predatory relations, made a claim on it. 'There will be just scrambled eggs,' he said, 'but that will be a change, which is always nice.' 'Yes,' I agreed, 'but next time couldn't Nadya have the change and let us have the buckwheat?'

But he was totally indifferent to food. Once he gave up his sugar ration for a whole month so that he could buy the works of Dorothy Wordsworth, of which a consignment had reached Leningrad.

One day the first snow came and the waters in the canals moved turbidly below a film of ice. Lihachev, who had been in Armenia, was back and we talked of going to ski at Pavlovsk. Everybody became cheerful and excited, the streets were gay and sparkling, and tiny children, so tightly buttoned into shubas that they looked like small sheep, pulled each other about in packing cases in the Yekaterinsky Sad. Once or twice a week we had free evenings and there were theatres and ballets and impromptu parties.

I was the only one who could buy at Torgsin, the foreign currency shop, but my black roubles were running out so I seldom went there or to the hotels. But for our parties I got bottles of sweet Caucasian wine. I had a pupil behind the counter who helped me dodge the queues. In the markets there was always plenty of bread, and different delicacies swept over the city in waves; honey or cheese or stiff black cranberry jam crowded the shops for a few weeks and then disappeared in a night as quickly as they had come. Instead came sock suspenders or celluloid tooth-brush cases and, in the window, a red cloth with a bust of Lenin on it. There were no containers for the honey and Kolya in his English mood refused to carry his jug in his hand down the Nevsky. Inevitably, Nina Gavrilovna blamed it on me that everything in his attaché case, books and lecture notes, were covered in honey.

Baroness Garatinsky came back from a visit to her son, who was imprisoned in Solovietsky Island; every day for five minutes she was allowed with all the other visitors into a long corridor, where behind an iron railing their relations were waiting to see them. So as to be heard, each tried to talk louder than his neighbour and, when it was impossible, they had to communicate by gestures. 'I felt we had stopped being human and become monkeys. Perhaps we have always been monkeys.'

Lihachev usually came with Yegunov, who taught English with him at the Marine Academy. He was a Greek scholar and had translated *Aethiopika*, a third-century Alexandrian novel by Heliodorus. As far as I could judge, Yegunov's translation and its ninety-page introduction would have brought him distinction in England. He was now translating Plato's *Timaeus*, also for the Academia Press, but hesitated to publish it. 'Two friends of mine,' he explained, 'were overheard at a party setting Plato above Karl Marx and they were banished from Leningrad.' 'Don't risk it then,' I said. 'Well, it was not so bad for them,' he answered doubtfully, 'they were unemployed stage managers and they were sent to Orel, where, as it happened, they got jobs straightaway in a new theatre. They sneak back to Leningrad, when they can. But I could not bear to leave Leningrad.' For though Leningrad is the least typical of Russian cities, its citizens love it as Parisians love Paris. They are unhappy away from its grave and charming avenues and gardens, its cold northern sunsets.

Yegunov had tuberculosis. Peter the Great built his city on a marsh for wealthy aristocrats with fur coats and servants with warming-pans and stoves, or else for tough mouzhiks, who would warm themselves with labour and vodka. A generation ago the remnants of a well-to-do bourgeoisie lived there without fuel or fur coats to interpose between themselves and the raw and foggy winters. How could they not get tuberculosis?

Lihachev was always cheerful. His father had been a wealthy doctor, who, at the outbreak of the Revolution, had invited all his relations and friends to share his two-storied house so that they need not have strangers forced on them. They had brought all their most cherished furniture with them. Two uncles had been in the consular service in Africa and had crammed the rooms with bamboo and bark and bronze and stamped leather. He told me that when they had all in the old days lived in different parts of Petrograd, they travelled long distances to quarrel with each other. 'Now it's so easy, there's no sport in it.'

One day in October we were eating raw herring and scrambled eggs, and having the last drop of the brandy flask I had brought from Ireland, when the telephone rang. It was a girl, in the flat above. She said she was a pupil of Kolya's at the Oriental Institute and, as they were having a party and short of 'cavaliers', would we come up and join them? Kolya said he had friends with him. 'Well, bring them all,' she said, so we all trooped upstairs.

The girl opened the door herself, but when she let go the doorhandle she slipped backwards and would have fallen if she had not clutched at Kolya. A girlfriend beside her was scarcely steadier on her feet and, when at last we got into the room, we saw the reason. It was an infinitely more luxurious flat than ours, with pre-revolutionary candelabras, family portraits and wall-hangings, and a long table heaped with grapes and pineapples, every variety of wine and liqueur and plates full of appetizing food. There were men in morning coats and ladies in evening dress. It was astonishing to come from our bleak, dark and damp quarters and to discover so much light and luxury a few feet above us, and in a room the same size and shape as ours. Half dazed, I flopped into a chair beside a plump lady with enormous ear-rings, who poured me out some curaçao and talked to me in faultless English about Ilfracombe. Then someone told me it was a wedding, and the bridegroom came and asked me very pleasantly to bring up my curaçao and come to dance in the next room. It was very small and corresponded to one of the factory workers' rooms down below. Lihachev was foxtrotting in the tiny floor and I found a partner and joined him. It was hot and uncomfortable and I sensed that something was wrong, but I could not tell what or why. Suddenly I discovered that the tension, which I had detected, was emanating in dense waves from Kolya, who sat scowling on a sofa beside Yegunov. My partner suggested that we should stop and sample some of the delicious food and I gratefully agreed. Then I saw Kolya talking in a very haughty way to a lady, who I assumed to be the hostess, and who looked embarrassed.

All at once he got up and swept us along with him in a puzzled, disapproving crocodile, making it difficult for us to say any thank-yous or goodbyes.

It was not until I got downstairs that I understood what had happened. The two girls, the bride and her friend, both of them Kolya's pupils and both drunk, had dared each other to ask their romantic-looking teacher to the wedding party. Brimfull of hospitality and alcohol, the bride had chortled excitedly down the telephone without thinking of consulting her Mama. She must have been appalled when, instead of the glittering cavaliers she expected, four frowsy intellectuals in shabby suits turned up. Lihachev was the best of us because he was still in his naval uniform. But the bride's mother, a dignified lady with grey hair, came up to Kolya and explained that there had been 'a little misunderstanding': 'We're not the sort of people, you know, who just ask anyone to our family functions.' Kolya had snapped back loudly that it was no pleasure for him to come but the bride had been so pressing on the telephone. A stunned silence of embarrassment fell on the wedding party for two minutes and then was skilfully dispelled by a tornado of convivial noises as we trooped away down the stairs.

Once or twice my pupils invited me to birthday parties. They were mostly easy and pleasant and uneventful. Why does one remember the embarrassing occasions best? There was Olga N. and her mother, bourgeois, still only half-adjusted to the new regime.

— *Peter's Window* —

Kolya and I arrived at her birthday party with a cake I had chosen with care at Torgsin, covered with crystallized cherries, and I was disappointed when Olga, not looking at it, grandly told the maid to put it with a pile of other unopened presents on the piano. She was a prize pupil of mine and prattled away in a low, quiet, self-important voice in very literary English. When we came in, the mother was saying, 'Oh dear, not enough teaspoons! Where can the wretched girl have put the spoons?' Olga then said to the company in English: 'My Mother had formerly four dozen teaspoons, but she was forced to sell three dozen. She is very old fashioned and now greatly regrets the deprivation and cannot reconcile herself to the loss. Consequently she resorts to little subterfuges such as you have just heard.' She herself was worried about the buttons on her blouse. The little red ornaments on them were wearing out, but, because they were enamel, couldn't be painted in, so she was getting a friend, a chemical engineer, to help. He was first of all going to scoop out the centres, and then . . .

These are the things we talked about in Leningrad in 1931: spoons, buttons, macaroni, galoshes, macaroni again. I don't believe I ever heard anyone mention Magnetogorsk or the liquidation of the Kulaks or any of the remote and monstrous contemporary happenings to which by a complicated chain of causes our lifestyle and our macaroni were linked.

Communism is said to inspire a dull uniformity,

but Lihachev, who was quite unpolitical, was always seeking and finding coloured variations. In his rooms I met Negro communists and Turks, Tartars and Kirghiz, and one day he took me to the Hispano-American Society. It was held in the room of a Mexican communist, a lady, who dreaded the Russian winter. In the autumn she had shut herself and her family into her room and sealed up the large double window and the phortochka; and then fought the domestic and personal smells with powerful scents. It was not yet mid-winter, but it was plain to all the battle had been lost. Lilies and jasmine had been routed by an appalling primeval smell that was neither Slav nor Latin. Lihachev said it was Aztec. The lady introduced me to a celebrated Mexican writer, but talking meant breathing, and I appeared to him to be dumb, and he went over to Lihachev. For Lihachev, as I heard long afterwards, it proved to be a disastrous meeting. The Mexican was charmed with him, and when he went home he sent his book on Communism for Lihachev to review. Unfortunately the book had Trotskyite tendencies and he was compromised by receiving it. He was dismissed from the navy and he became a literary freelance compiling anthologies of foreign poetry, always lively and occupied. In a large new sombrero, he visited all the Leningrad publishing houses and got contracts.

That was the last I heard of him, but before I left Leningrad Vera Garatinksy had told me that in a couple of years there would be enough English-speaking proletarians to replace all the bourgeois teachers and guides and translators. That will be the end of us,' she said. 'It's that accursed English woman and her method. Don't let them invent any more clever methods over there, please.'

My way to Goskurs lay along the Moika, the little river that ran from the Winter Palace under the Nevsky and the Vosnesensky to the Neva. It had been a very aristocratic district once. On the far side, in a pale green eighteenth-century house, Pushkin had lived and had died painfully after a fatal duel. The quays and surrounding streets were almost deserted in the winter evenings, and very quiet except for my galoshes slapping loosely on the pavements. In the marsh air the northern sunset quivered from time to time as if it was trapped between the beautiful impassive houses. In the daytime the red proletarian trimmings held the eye and the mind, but in the twilight different obsessions replaced them.

Before I went to Russia, I had been reading Dostoyevsky's *The Idiot*. It is the story of passionate people pursuing each other through the streets of St Petersburg, with love, with hate, with revolvers or bundles of roubles. Their feelings and their motives are often obscure, and Dostoyevsky, standing outside his own creations, suggests different explanations of their behaviour. Through this, his characters have the freshness of reality, for mostly we only guess at other peoples' minds. Prince Mishkin, the Idiot, is the still centre of the hurricane, the personification of Dostoyevsky's belief that 'the Russian heart is more adapted to universal brotherly friendship than that of any other nation'. And indeed perhaps the Russians are more perceptive and, when it is in their power, more ready than others to make allowances for the failures they perceive. The first people to give Prince Mishkin hospitality, when he arrived poor and shabby in St Petersburg, were the Yepanchins, who lived in a large house on the broad bustling Sadovaya, where I caught the tram for my classes. Mishkin was at peace with himself and, despite his simplicity, this gave him a strange authority over others. To Dostoyevsky he was the symbol of Russia's unconscious, unexercised power.

I do not believe that the creations of genius die without issue or that, because of a change of government, cities start to breed a different type of man. They dress differently, and feed differently, and that is all.

Great writers interpret men to each other by example and analogy. The creative imagination ebbs and flows with some degree of constancy. On the one hand all men have common needs, passions, hopes, which society has to satisfy; on the other hand every man is unique and he must so manipulate society that his nature is fulfilled. The great Russian writers, Tolstoy, Dostoyevsky, Chekhov, were almost always more conscious of diversity of temperament than of uniformity of needs. Then Karl Marx and the Revolution created

— *Peter's Window* —

the Economic Man, and while this wonderfully life-like dummy is in the shop window, what hope is there for the genius that is kindled by human diversity? The fact that there are vast editions of the classics published and sold out keeps the flame alive but cannot fan it.

I once tried to talk about these things at Goskurs during the dangerous half-hour of free conversation, when my pupils and I, under cover of grammar, tried to find out what we were like. One of them helped me out with a cliché, 'ghosts of the past', which quenched what I had to say, and instead I said that Petersburg, like Alexandria and Constantinople, had the tremendous toughness of cities that were built round an idea, not a market. Peter's 'window upon Europe' had been made for autocrats and bureaucrats, but once opened it could not be shut. Marx came through as well as Dickens and Byron and Georges Sand and Henry George and all the strange assortment of foreign influences. Tolstoy, no less than Dostoyevsky the Slavophile, had hated Petersburg and its Western culture, as the oyster hates the foreign body it turns into a pearl, but they could not ignore it. And what they had accepted and adorned, their successors could still less ignore.

The weather was getting foggy. Most Russians had sealed up their windows, but whenever I shut the phortochka Kolya opened it again. Fresh air was one of his cherished English traditions, about which he was very sensitive. His love of England was a substitute for religion and I knew that his welcome to me derived from it. There was a legend in Techmass about his 'English reserve', but in fact there was nothing English about it. He was normally impetuous and enthusiastic but in his English mood he alternated between a cold animal torpor and a passionate misanthropy. 'English dissent and socialism,' I said, 'are based on an accidental tepidity or, if you like, sobriety of temperament. Your emotional heterodoxy is something quite different.' I would not have risked saying this but my cold was getting worse and I was scared of getting stranded in Leningrad with bronchitis. The next time I shut the phortochka he looked stern but left it shut.

Once, when I was sitting over my sudak in the October, an Oxford acquaintance, John Lane-Tuckey and his wife, a sleek, self-satisfied university couple, came by. They were tired of crêches and clinics and wanted to see 'real Russians'. It seemed obvious to ask them back and Kolya was pleased. But the moment they came into the room I saw it was a mistake. John asked light ironical questions about Soviet economics – he was a sociologist. Barbara, his wife, was silent, clearly horrified by the squalor of the flat. Something in their manner and appearance turned Kolya into a pillar of Marxist orthodoxy. His open friendliness dropped and he talked to them as if he was giving copy to journalists. I took them back to their hotel. 'But you can't go on living there,' Barbara Lane-Tuckey said, 'the smell, the dark!' She was kind and worried and pressed on me what they'd brought from England and no longer needed, a packet of lump sugar, three lemons and a bottle of hydrogen peroxide to gargle. I felt unsettled, like a child at school who has had a visit from home. I tried to come back into the flat as if it was for the first time, so as to experience what they had seen and Smelt. Yes, it was unbelievable. I shut up the provisions in my trunk. Neither of us referred to the Lane-Tuckeys again.

Kolya had appalling moments of self-criticism. Soon after this he stayed up a whole night reading *A Passage to India.* Closing the book at breakfast-time, he said, 'I'm like Aziz. I'm an Asiatic.' He was sombre the entire day, but he felt he had given himself away too much, for a little later he started to refer to Lyubotchka as 'the maid' and to give her lessons in waiting at table. She was always terrified of him when he was being English. He instructed her in a cool, bitter, military voice: 'All over again till you get it right, please.' Lyubotchka reacted as if to electric shocks. She started to jerk and dart about like a rabbit, her eyes glazed with fear. Eating, which she had done all her life, suddenly became black magic.

When I found someone had been rummaging in my suitcase, I kept count of the lumps of sugar and chocolate, and found two or three pieces disappeared every day. They were precious as gold to me in case I

— THE INVADER WORE SLIPPERS —

got ill and couldn't go out to buy food. Nina Gavrilovna used to do all their shopping in the market, and if I asked her to go to Torgsin, the foreign currency shop, people might think she had been receiving valuta from abroad or hoarding jewellery.

One day a golden-haired cousin of Kolya's called, all charm and friendliness, but Kolya was nervous and abrupt. He obviously wanted her to go, but she stayed on. At last she turned to me and said, 'I wonder if . . . ?' Kolya shot up into the air and came between us, clenching his fists: 'No, that I forbid you to ask him! That you shall not ask! No!' She shrugged her shoulders and left, followed by Kolya raging. The hall door slammed. After a bit the girl came back with a bottle in her hand. 'I wanted to ask you if I could have a drop of peroxide for my hair?'

When Kolya came back I told him that she was welcome to my peroxide but I thought Lyubotchka was stealing things out of my trunk. He became very solemn: 'The matter must be brought before the House Committee.' That evening the curtain flapped ceaselessly over his mother's recess. The murmur of conversation never ceased. When Kolya went out, she emerged and asked me if I wasn't ashamed, a greedy foreigner, who cheated on the currency and had fine meals in the Europa, to count lumps of sugar and persecute a poor servant-girl? And I had lemons in my trunk too, and chocolate.

'How did you know I had lemons in my trunk?'

— *Peter's Window* —

I couldn't stop myself asking. Oh, she crowed, she'd been digging in my trunk, had she? What would Kolya say when he heard I accused his mother of being a thief? This I could not answer. My Russian was not good enough for me to pick my way through the tangle of misunderstandings. 'And Kolya has given up his translating in order to show you the way round Leningrad. You don't even pay for your lodgings.'

I tried to explain the arrangement Kolya and I had come to, adding, 'Perhaps he didn't fully understand?'

'So he didn't understand? He can't understand English can he? He speaks it as well as you do, if not better. That'll be news to him he can't speak English.' And then she produced her trump card. 'If the GPU knew you have black roubles . . . Russians have been shot for less!'

At this moment the Pole came to the door. He was very apologetic for interrupting and sincerely anxious that we go on with our quarrel and not mind him. Nina Gavrilovna went out and he produced a slip of paper and explained to me how many weeks I had earned by my translations to use his aunt's bed. But chiefly he had come to ask me to a party. He gave a ceremonious bow. It was for the Fifteenth Anniversary of the Revolution; it was going to be a very special party. I accepted and he told me I would get a formal invitation in a day or two. I had an almost permanent cold now and I kept on wondering what would happen if either the aunt or I got ill. I wished I had paid more attention to the conducted tours around infirmaries and hospitals.

When Kolya came home that night, his mother drew him behind her curtain. Then I heard him leave. He did not come back that night or the following morning. Then the telephone started to ring as it had the first day I spent in Chernyshev Pereulok, and I answered the pupils as his mother had done, 'Ne doma. Ne znaioo.'

He came back in the evening. 'I can't stay in the house with you any longer,' he said. 'I'm going to Lihachev's.' He began to pack a suitcase.

'If you think I'm to blame, I'll go.'

'You've nowhere to go.'

'I'll find somewhere!' I jumped up and put on my coat and hat and, seizing my suitcase, walked out of the room.

Kolya was out of his mind. 'That's my coat,' he said. 'I can't trust you to bring it back. You must leave your suitcase behind instead.'

I threw the suitcase down and flung the coat at him too, in a rage. When I was half-way down the stairs, the door of the flat opened and his mother came running after me. 'Come back,' she said, 'he just lost his temper. He hasn't had anything to eat all day.'

'No, I won't come back.'

'Please come back. If the GPU hears that Kolya turned you out, he'll get into trouble.'

'They won't hear.'

— *Peter's Window* —

It was not until I was in the street that I realized I had left my passport in Kolya's coat, but nothing would have induced me to return.

Leningrad was very badly lit in the evenings and the directions hard to follow, as the new street names were usually too long to use. The Nevsky, for example, was never called its proper name, October Twenty-Fifth Street. At so late an hour I hesitated to go to Yegunov, who lived nearby. He had a single room in a vast tenement house, honeycombed with arches and passages, the entries blocked with stacks of firewood and stinking rubbish-heaps, and every arch and entry looked alike. The Pole's house was on the outskirts of the city in the Narva district, and I knew I would never find it.

There was a thin coat of snow in the Nevsky that flung back the light of the lamps. All the passers-by had on shubas, or leather coats, except for a few beggars in the archways and the old general standing as always with his tray of transfers and celluloid toothbrush-cases outside the Moscow Station. Yet in spite of the snow I was so angry and excited I did not feel cold. I walked up and down the Nevsky enquiring at all the hotels, big and small. They would none of them take me. They were full up with delegates from the provinces for the Fifteenth Anniversary. In any case, as I was registered in a private house, I would have first to get my registration cancelled at the police station, and that had closed three hours earlier. At the Gostiny Dvor, the big shopping-centre between the Nevsky and the Sadovya, I ate some pirozhkies, hot cabbage pies, at a stall. There were lights in the Kazan Cathedral, where the finishing touches were being put to an historical exhibition, and outside workmen on scaffolding were nailing up strips of red cloth for the celebrations. Some others were sitting round a brazier eating food out of parcels.

Opposite the Kazan Cathedral was the British Consulate. Mr Bullard, whom I knew, got his food from a London shop. He had deep armchairs and a roaring fire. Several times I had dropped in for a chat and a cup of tea and Huntley and Palmer chocolate biscuits. He was friendly but did not approve, any more than the Russians did, of fraternization. Kolya told me that he had tried to take Connie Archangelsky's passport from her because she was married to a Russian. Rumour said that there was always someone lurking by the cathedral steps making a note of his visitors. He had good manners and would be able to dissemble his satisfaction at seeing somebody paid out for staying in a Russian family. He himself only met official Russians and had to go to Finland to get Russian lessons.

I could easily persuade myself that I had an official claim on him, but I loathed going to him, as I would to the GPU. I thought I had the courage and skill to treat most human problems as personal ones, but the moment I appealed to authority to help me out I was like a man on a tightrope who thinks of falling. Could I convince myself that the consul was a friend as well as an official? I hesitated and all at once the light went out in the consulate. My mind was made up.

I rang the bell on the first landing, but there was no answer. I rang again and knocked. After half an hour of waiting I came down into the street. I walked on towards the Admiralty and sweeping aside by St Isaac's I tried the Astoria and finally ended up on the Neva. It was no good. When I got back to the Kazan Cathedral I was shivering with cold and the workmen round the brazier whom I intended to ask for a night's lodgings had gone. I walked back to the consulate and banged at all the doors in the building. Bullard emerged from one of them. 'You were knocking at the offices, which closed at four,' he explained. 'The private part of the house is on this side.'

I had no self-reproaches as I got into bed, for I was persuaded that I was going to be desperately ill.

The next morning I woke up feeling remarkably well. I had an English breakfast with eggs and bacon, marmalade and toast and coffee. Afterwards I went out and bought the commissar's coat with the short sleeves. The sun was shining. The palaces on the canals, freshly colour-washed in buff or pink, were framed in snow and draped with broad red banners. I felt wonderfully detached from it all. The palaces wore their banners with the patient suffering look of domestic pets wearing bows for a birthday party. About everything there was an impromptu, impermanent and almost innocent look.

It was with a feeling of insolent well-being that I returned to Chernishev Pereulok. After I had rung the bell I felt ashamed of my new coat and folded it into a bundle. Kolya was in bed. We were polite and constrained. He handed me a postcard from Vaishlé, the Pole. 'Gubert Georgievitch. Congratulations on the Fifteenth Anniversary of Socialist Construction and the termination of the fourth year of the five-year plan! I also invite you to my house for the latter half of tomorrow, the first day of the holidays.'

The kitchen was full of smoke, for everybody in the flat was having a bath for the Anniversary. No one trusted the cleanliness of the bath itself but put a stool inside and balanced a basin of hot water on the stool. Darya Andreyvna even placed in it a trough for her feet. I used to prefer to wash in the communal baths, where there was constant hot water and elderly people lashed themselves with birch twigs.

Darya Andreyvna was going to lead the procession for the theatre. Kolya was marching for the Oriental Institute. The Director of Techmass had rung up to find if I would march with them, but I had been out and did not know where to meet them. Kolya, instead of being flippant as he usually was about processions, was important and treated me as if I was Lane-Tuckey. I would never be forgiven that night at the consulate. As we went out he made a stately, unfriendly apology. He had been in a Manichean mood, he said. He insisted that I should come back that night. I agreed I would and said that I would see that his wife Connie in Eastbourne would get the same rent that he had to pay when he worked for the Soviet Embassy and lived in Torrington Square, but I said I must have the phortochka shut. We discussed the matter in a business-like way, as if Chernishev Pereulok was in fact a Bloomsbury lodging-house.

As we were going down the stairs we met the Pole coming up. He had a big peony in his buttonhole with slogans stamped in gold on each petal. 'I came to see if you had got my invitation', he said. 'Yes, and I'm coming.' 'Good! And I brought you this.'

It was another letter. Handing it to me, he bolted down the stairs and disappeared. When I unstuck it, a packet of roubles tumbled out with a note: 'Lent for an indefinite period, in case you are short for the celebration of the Fifteenth Anniversary of Socialist Construction.' I went to Torgsin and bought some bottles of wine to take to the party.

It was difficult pressing my way through the crowds in the Nevsky and, at the corner of the Sadovya, I was brought to a halt by a fresh tributary coming in from the Neva docks and the English Quay. I had to wait there wedged against a parapet for several hours. I was told that a million men and women passed along the Nevsky that day. In each group of this endless procession two men on either flank held up a flapping red streamer with a slogan on it, or grotesque figures of European statesmen. It was fully an hour before the students' and teachers' procession passed. I wanted to see if there was anyone I knew, and how they were affected by this performance. Organized in processions, those whom we have known as complex individuals shed colour and character. Also there is some unconscious tabu that we violate every time we look at our friends in their public moments, which are often the moments of deepest privacy. The violation may be easy and pleasant, but it delays us for that split second between perceiving and observing. Kolya passed close by but not till he had gone did I realize that I had seen him. A column of sailors went by and I looked in vain for Lihachev. A little later I noticed a dislocation in the procession, people moderating their step behind and on either side of the baroness. She walked slowly enough for me to watch her. Her companions on either side, keeping step, held a pole from which a banner was stretched: WE ARE MARCHING TOWARDS THE CONQUEST OF TECHNICAL EFFICIENCY IN A SOCIALIST WORLD. She did not look either ironical or embarrassed. It was as if she was half asleep but sufficiently awake to enjoy her dream. She did not seem conscious of her lameness, imposing her pace with confidence on those around her.

I have thought that just as half our physical lives passes in sleep, it is perhaps intended that our mental life should be equally distributed between the assertion of our uniqueness and its renunciation. If that trance-like state of submersion in a public or collective mood bears an analogy to sleep, it would reflect our individual and self-centred lives by very simple images and phrases in dream-like sequences. In such a way, the caricatures and slogans that floated above them would complement, like dreams, the intricate, logical natures of Kolya and the baroness. The slogans were the shadows of human thinking in which their thoughts merged restfully, just as their footsteps concurred in the broad beaten track upon the snow, and we do not expect faithfulness in tone or form or colour from shadows.

All I remember of the Pole's party is the food and a tall thin guest with a bald head, a geologist like Vaishlé. As he shook hands, he said, 'I am bald and thin because I think very much; my Polish friend is round and jolly because he never thinks. I have been prospecting in Turkestan and I will show you some photographs. Later still I will recite you some poems of the French poet, Béranger.' All happened as he predicted. As for the food, there were golubtsi (mince and rice wrapped in cabbage leaves and fried), hard cakes covered with stewed apple, soft cakes covered with poppy seeds, glasses of vodka mixed with lemonade and chilis. I saw the aunt and her bed, but I had decided to leave Russia and the desperate significance they would have had for me a week before was no longer there.

The last few weeks before the schools closed I spent at Chernishev Pereulok. Kolya submerged himself in his translation of Lenin and began to take his Communism and his professional functions much more seriously. I was a foreign critic now not a friend and he would step coldly from argument to argument, like rungs on a ladder. His English obsession only flared up now and again, as when every Saturday he laid a neat bill on my bed for me to forward to my wife. Several times, we made up parties to Sestroretsk or Pavlovsk or Gatchina. He was never unfriendly but he had become a different person, conscientious, informative and rather dull. He provoked in me all the qualities I had detested in the Lane-Tuckeys.

I took many solitary walks under the lovely alleys of lime and maple round Leningrad. Lihachev was away but sometimes Yegunov came with me. He had a big dog which was in the stud book and therefore had a ration book of its own, and despite the rigours of the Five-Year Plan ate more than its master. We usually exercised it in the Kamenny Ostrov, the island in the Neva, where the wealthy merchant families, whose houses are now resthomes and hospitals, once lived. It was criss-crossed by little birch-lined canals and bridges. Sometimes I went with one or two of my pupils to the Yussupov Palace, to which as a teacher I had access. It was a Students' Recreation Centre, with rooms for chess and cards and billiards. It had also a small theatre. Down in the basement in the winter of 1916 Rasputin, who was hard to kill, was beaten to death by Prince Yussupov and his companions. The vast china chandelier in the hall surely dated from those days. There were robins and canaries perched on its branches, which dripped with blue convolvulus.

For my last evening Kolya decided to have a party and, setting enough money aside for my droshki to the station, I gave him the remainder of my roubles. I was pleased when he said, 'I will arrange it all,' and then spent more than half on smoked fish, a favourite delicacy of his. It was like a return to ordinary humanity. Lihachev was back home again and when our guests had gone in the early morning, he and Yegunov spread their shubas on the floor and slept on them. My train left very early, so I did not bother to sleep. Kolya and I left without rousing the others.

At the station, the Pole and Guzelimian and Tihomirov and two of my pupils were waiting. The Pole gave me a box of liqueur chocolates, Guzelimian asked me to remember his fishing-rod. Then there suddenly flashed into my mind, 'My blue carriage rug!' I exclaimed aloud, and promptly Kolya said, 'I'll fetch it!' and darted away. I shouted after him, 'For God's sake keep it!' but I paused for one greedy moment before I said this and I was too late. The blue rug, which I had brought from Ireland, had stood between me and pneumonia; now it meant nothing to me, but it could have meant a great deal to the Archangelskys. They got it in the end, but how ungraciously.

I kept looking at the station entrance while the others were talking, because I was wondering how I could keep in touch with my Russian friends. Would it be safe to write letters to each other? Could we send newspapers? I had left all this to the last moment, for I intended to ask Kolya and hear him say, 'I will arrange.' But the train went out. Alexander Ivanitch and the Pole looked at the wheels, which meant, I had been told, that they wanted me to come back.

The train went through lonely swamp, thinly wooded with birch and alder. Here and there a solitary Soviet soldier guarded the line until, as we approached the frontier, the main roads slowly became cart tracks and petered out into grass and barbed-wire entanglements.

* * *

In the autumn of 1956 I went with seven other Irishmen on a 'cultural delegation' to China. On the way back I parted from the others in Moscow because I wished to go to Leningrad to see if any of my old friends were alive. As the translator of Leonov's *The Thief*, I had good contacts with the Union of Writers and, when I told them my reasons for wishing to go to Leningrad, I met with understanding. They said they would look out for a guide to take me on the night train the following day. But would I in the meantime give them a talk on Irish Writing? I went back to the Hotel National and spent the day in my room writing and was ready for my appointment with them in the afternoon. There were about a dozen people there, mostly teachers and

— *Peter's Window* —

translators. They asked me searching and intelligent questions. One of them was translating O'Casey's autobiographical series and he asked me to interpret a passage in O'Casey's idiosyncratic idiom, which always seemed to me to obscure what was otherwise lucid. I did badly but recovered a little of my credit when I said that in *Sunset and Evening Star* O'Casey had written a couple of friendly pages about me and the 'Insult' to the Papal Nuncio.

As I left them I was told that my guide, Anna Shelestova, would meet me at the National late that evening and take me on the night train to Leningrad. On the train I reflected on my chances of finding any of my friends alive. There was only a thin hope. What I had heard as rumour at home had been confirmed in Moscow. In 1934, three years after I had left, Kirov, the Leningrad Party Boss, whom many thought would be Stalin's successor, had been murdered. Foreign influence was suspected and many thousands of arrests were made on the flimsiest of evidence. I heard how the elderly vet who treated the German consul's dog, and the woman who sold eggs to the Polish consul, had been hauled off to prison. It was obvious that all foreign-language teachers would be under suspicion. Five years later the war had broken out, and after that came the invasion of Russia and the terrible siege of Leningrad. It was a forlorn hope.

Almost all my friends in Leningrad had had telephones, so the first thing we did when we arrived was to look up their names in the telephone book. Only one familiar name was there, the one I most wanted to see, Nikolai Mihalitch Archangelsky. He was not in Chernishev Pereulok but in the southern suburb of Narva. When Anna telephoned, a female voice said that he was out but would be back at two.

We leapt into a cab and, as Anna was a native of Leningrad, we quickly found the Archangelsky's flat. It was in a large new tenement block and No. 32 was on the third storey. When the door was opened by a big blowsy woman, there was a babel of children's voices and kitchen smells. She did not ask us in but said that if we cared to wait, Nikolai Mihalitch would be along in twenty minutes. 'Does he still work at the Oriental Institute?' I asked. 'No, he works at the Kirov Factory.' 'That was the Putilov in your time,' interjected Anna. 'Does he write at all now?' I asked. The woman looked puzzled. 'He's an engineer,' she said. It took me a moment to grasp that there were two Nikolai Mihalitch Archangelskys, and that this was the wrong one. I could not stay there a second longer. 'Let's at least try Chernishev Pereulok,' I said to Anna. My disappointment had turned into relief, for the Nikolai Mihalitch I knew would have been miserable in such surroundings.

I was no help to Anna in finding our way to Chernishev Pereulok. All the familiar landmarks had gone, and when we arrived and stopped at No. 59 I got out in perplexity. Even in the hallway it was different. The lift was working. Could these be the stairs that I had

— *Peter's Window* —

run down with Nina Gavrilovna shouting after me that night I had spent at the consul's? It was not possible. We went up in the lift all the same and stopped on the fifth floor.

Darya Andreyevna's mirror had gone and so had the mat. A stranger came to the door when I rang the bell. No, he had never heard of anyone called Nikolai Mihalitch Archangelsky, but there was a very old lady in the flat still who had been there since before the war. She might know. 'Is it Darya Andreyevna?' I asked. 'Yes, that's her name.' I described myself and he said he would find out if she would see me. He came back and said the old lady remembered me – an Englishman – but she was bedridden and did not want to see a strange man; she'd see the woman who came with me. So Anna went alone. I waited for a long time on the landing till Anna came out. She said Darya Andreyevna remembered the Archangelskys well. The mother had died and sometime in the mid-thirties Nikolai Mihalitch had been taken away to Gorohovaia Prison for quite a short period. He had come back and after three weeks had died in the flat.

I could not leave it like that. It seemed to me that Tihomirov, as a Red Army man, was the one who was likely to have survived the purge that followed Kirov's murder. By a strange chance I had in my notebook the number of the two old women with whom he lodged, and in a moment I was talking to the one who had survived. Yes, she remembered Alexander Ivanitch talking about me, the Englishman. 'Poor Alexander Ivanitch! He died you know three years ago. I always told him he drank too much coffee.' This seemed a very old-ladyish diagnosis, but I asked her did she remember Lihachev and Yegunov and Kolya. Indeed she did, but Alexander Ivanitch had not been seeing anything of them for a very long time before he died. 'How long?' 'Oh, maybe fifteen or twenty years ago. I think something may have happened to them.' She was not going to tell me more and maybe she did not know. When anyone went to prison in those days, their relations used to bring them parcels, until one day they were told no more parcels were necessary. You were not informed whether they had died or been moved to another prison.

I had learnt very much what I had expected to learn, which was nothing. I was sad not only for my friends but for anyone who leaves the world anonymously, surrounded by hostile or uncaring people.

Anna had done her best for me. There was still half a day. What would I like to see? I did not want to go sight-seeing, and in any case most of the Intourist sights had been destroyed by the Germans. The imperial palaces in the southern environs of the city, Peterhov, Gatchina, Pavlovsk, Tsarskoye Selo, had all lain in the path of the German advance and had been looted and burned. All the trees in their parks had been cut down. 'But we're restoring them,' said Anna, loyal to Intourism, 'and we're getting all the pictures and sculptures back again, or their equivalents. And we've replanted the trees.'

In the end she took me to a hill overlooking the city and the Gulf of Finland. There was a slot-machine telescope there and with a running commentary from Anna I turned it round. To the west I saw the island of Kronstadt and the wooded coast of Finland, and Anna told me how, backed by the Finns, the Germans had flung forty-five divisions against the city. After the victory at Kingisepp, in which her brother had died, they forced their way across the Estonian frontier, confident that the city would fall to them in a couple of days, but the siege had lasted twenty-nine months and had ended in a Russian victory. Moving the telescope towards the city, I saw the Nevsky Prospekt thrusting eastwards to the Champs de Mars. The biggest fire from the incendiary bombs, Anna said, had been in the Gostiny Dvor. That was the shopping-centre in the Nevsky where I had eaten pirozhkies the night I slept at the consulate. She told me about the famine and how her brother's family had eaten carpenter's glue and yeast with hot water, till the fierce winter of 1941–42 when they had made a road across the ice on Lake Ladoga and transported food across from the east. I traced the Neva till it veered southwards by the Finland Station and the Summer Palace. To the north I saw the islands where I had walked with Yegunov and his dog. They were now called the Kirov Islands, Anna told me, and the great highway that led to them was called Kirov Avenue.

Thousands of honest men and women died because of Kirov, but their names are nowhere recorded.

I have forgotten much of what Anna told me but I am more inclined to apologize for writing about great events, which touched me not at all, than for tracing again the tiny snail track which I made myself.

Is it not obvious that when through the modern media far things are brought near, the near things must be pushed far to make room for them? Imperceptibly, we become Lilliputians wandering in a Brobdignag of our own contrivances and persuading ourselves that through contact with greatness we ourselves become greater. Then something happens to jerk us back to thoughts and people of our own size and significance. Most of the time when I was looking through that telescope, I was thinking not of the tremendous disasters that had befallen Leningrad and all Russia, but of the small stupidities, the acts of laziness or greed I had committed myself. Why had I not given the blue rug to Kolya's mother instead of leaving it behind by mistake? Why hadn't I sent Guzelimian his fishing-rod?

– The Artukovitch File –
[1985]

I. REFLECTIONS ON A CROATIAN CRUSADE

Some years after I had written 'The Sub-Prefect Should Have Held His Tongue', I was in New York and read how the Yugoslav Government was urging that Artukovitch, Pavelitch's Minister of the Interior, who was living in California, should be extradited. I went to the Yugoslav Consulate to enquire about this and was handed a fat yellow booklet called *Artukovitch, the Himmler of Yugoslavia* by three New Yorkers called Gaffney, Starchevitch and McHugh.

Artukovitch first won notoriety in October 1934. He had gone to England at the time of King Alexander's murder at Marseilles. After his visit to Paris, the king had intended to see his son, Crown Prince Peter, at Sandroyd School, so, in case the Marseilles attempt failed, Artukovitch had been deputed to arrange for the king's assassination in England. It did not fail so Artukovitch waited in Czechoslovakia and Hungary till the Nazi invasion of Yugoslavia. He then returned with them and held various ministerial posts under Pavelitch from 1944 to 1945 in the Independent State of Croatia. Very few people have heard of him, yet if his story were told with remorseless candour, we would have a picture not only of Croatia forty years ago, but of all Christendom in our century. Everything that the New Yorkers relate was already known to me, except for one startling paragraph, an extract from a memoir by Artukovitch himself. After describing how he escaped to Austria and Switzerland in 1945, he goes on:

I stayed in Switzerland until July 1947. Then with the knowledge of the Swiss Ministry of Justice I obtained personal documents for myself and my family, which enabled us to travel to Ireland. Using the name of Anitch, we stayed there until 15th July, 1948. When our Swiss documents expired, the Irish issued new papers and under Irish papers we obtained a visa for entry into the USA.

So evidently we in Ireland had sheltered this notable man for a whole year. He was not, like Eichmann, a humble executive, but himself a maker of history, dedicated to the extermination not of Jews alone, but also of his fellow-Christians, the Serbian Orthodox. He was a member of the govenment which in the spring of 1941 introduced laws which expelled them from Zagreb, confiscated their property and imposed the death penalty on those who sheltered them. Some twenty concentration camps were established in which they were exterminated. Why do we know so little about his sojourn among us? Did he stay in a villa at Foxrock or in lodgings at Bundoran or in some secluded midland cloister? And who looked after him? The Red Cross?

— *The Artukovitch File* —

And did we cherish him because he presented himself to us as a Christian refugee from godless Communism? That seems to me rather likely.

Nowadays we usually estimate cruelty by statistics and Gaffney and Co. use the figures normally recorded for Croatia by Jewish and Orthodox writers, that is to say, 30,000 Jews and 750,000 Orthodox massacred, 240,000 Orthodox forcibly converted to Catholicism. Even if these figures are exaggerated, it was the most bloodthirsty religio-racial crusade in history, far surpassing anything achieved by Cromwell and the Spanish Inquisitors. I am sorry that Gaffney and Co. give so many photographs of headless babies, of disembowelled shopkeepers, of burning beards soaked in kerosene, for Artukovitch.was, like Himmler, a 'desk-murderer', who deplored the disorderly and sadistic way in which his instructions were carried out. He was respectable, and it is the correlation of respectability and crime that nowadays has to be so carefully investigated.

The three writers tell Artukovitch's story with much emotion, because, as is plain, they want him to be extradited and hanged. But in itself the story is of the highest importance, for no earlier crusade has been so richly documented. If the abundant material were coolly and carefully studied, how much could we learn about human weakness and hypocrisy! We could observe how adroitly religion can be used in the service of crime. When Pavelitch and Artukovitch and their armies retreated, they were sure that, on the defeat of Germany, England and America would turn upon Russia and they could return to Zagreb. Therefore nothing was destroyed, the state documents were stored in the Archepiscopal Palace, the gold (dentures, wrist-watches and all) was hidden below the deaf and dumb confessional in the Franciscan monastery and cemented over by the friars themselves. The newspapers of the time, secular and ecclesiastical, are still to be seen in the Municipal Library, but this huge pile of documents, the Rosetta Stone of Christian corruption, has not yet been effectively deciphered.

These terrible Church papers, 1941 to 1945, should destroy forever our faith in those diplomatic prelates, often good and kindly men, who believe that at all costs the ecclesiastical fabric, its schools and rules, its ancient privileges and powers, should be preserved. The clerical editors published the Aryan laws, the accounts of the forced conversions, without protest, the endless photographs of Pavelitch's visits to seminaries and convents and the ecstatic speeches of welcome with which he was greeted. Turn, for example, to *Katolicki Tjednik (The Catholic Weekly)*, Christmas 1941, and read the twenty-six-verse 'Ode to Pavelitch', in which Archbishop Sharitch praises him for his measures against Serbs and Jews. Examine the Protestant papers and you will find the same story. Is it not clear that in times like those the Church doors should be shut, the Church newspapers closed down, and Christians, who believe that we should love our

— *The Artukovitch File* —

neighbours as ourselves, should go underground and try to build up a new faith in the catacombs?

Why did our professional historians not deal with all this long ago? They seem to wait till history is dead before they dare to touch it. But does a good surgeon only operate on corpses? They have wholly misinterpreted their functions, for it is their duty to expose the liar before his contagion has spread. While Artukovitch was on his way to Ireland, a Dublin publication told us authoritatively that the massacre of the Serbian Orthodox had never happened. In Count O'Brien's book* on Mgr Stepinac, to which I have already referred, we read:

They [the Orthodox] were offered by Pavelitch the choice between conversion to the Catholic faith or death . . . But the Catholic Church as a whole, all her bishops and the overwhelming majority of her priests, led by the Archbishop of Zagreb, made this evil plan impossible.

Some of the correspondence between Artukovitch and Stepinac has been published in English by Richard Pattee[†] and, collating with Gaffney, we see how Stepinac, a brave and merciful though very simple man, was hopelessly compromised by his official connection with the state. It was only his own flock whom he could

* A. H. O'Brien, *Archbishop Stepinac, The Man and His Case* (London 1947).
[†] Richard Pattee, *The Case of Cardinal Aloysius Stepinac* (London/Milwaukee 1953).

help, and even them very little. For example, he appealed to Artukovitch on behalf of one of his priests, Father Rihar, who had defied Pavelitch. His failure was absolute, for this is how Artukovitch replied:

Zagreb. 17th November, 1942. In connection with your esteemed request of 2nd November, 1942 . . . notice is hereby given that Francis Rihar by the decree of this office of 20th April, 1942, No. 26417/1942, was sentenced to forced detention in the concentration camp at Jasenovac for a period of three years . . . because as pastor at Gornja Stubica he did not celebrate a solemn high mass on the anniversary of the founding of the Independent State of Croatia . . . nor did he consent to sing the psalm *Te Deum Laudamus,* saying that it was nowhere prescribed in ecclesiastical usage . . .

Stepinac appealed again, but Rihar had been already three months at Jasenovac and, therefore, according to the rules of this camp, he was killed.

How, anyway, could Stepinac defend Father Rihar with any authority, since he himself had done what Rihar refused to do? Gaffney and Co., on page 42, reproduced seven photographs of the celebration of Pavelitch's birthday on 15 June 1942, and a letter from the Archbishop exhorting his clergy to hold a *Te Deum* after High Mass the following Sunday, 17 June, because of 'Our Glorious Leader'.

Since Pattee omitted this very relevant letter, it is strange that he printed Stepinac's correspondence with Artukovitch about the Jews, for this makes it clear that in acknowledging the authority of Pavelitch, the Archbishop, for diplomatic reasons, felt obliged to accept the terminology of the anti-semites and their human classifications. For example, on 30 May 1941 he urged Artukovitch 'to separate the Catholic non-Aryans from non-Christian non-Aryans in relation to their social position and in the manner of treating them'.

Much has been written about Communist distortions of history, but only recently has our own inability, as Christians, to report facts honestly been closely investigated. Now, after twenty years, the dam has burst and the truth, a turbid stream, is inundating our self-complacency and irrigating our self-knowledge. Catholic scholars are leading the way. For example, Professor Gordon Zahn has shown how selective is the documentation on which the biographies of Christian heroes of the resistance are based. Their sermons and speeches were pruned of all the compliments they paid to Hitler and his New Order and no row of dots in the text marks the excision of these now-embarrassing ecstasies.

In the long run, remorseless truth-telling is the best basis for ecumenical harmony. Hitler once explained to Hermann Rauschning how he intended to use the Churches as his propagandists. 'Why should we quarrel? They will swallow anything provided they can keep their material advantages.' Yet Hitler never succeeded in corrupting the Churches as effectively as did Pavelitch and Artukovitch, who professed to be Christians. We shall not be able to estimate the extent of their success and how it might have been resisted, while a single fact is diplomatically 'forgotten'. It is well known that those who suppress history have to relive it.

* * *

How did Artukovitch (alias Anitch) get to Ireland? I wrote to Yugoslavia, to America, France, Germany and questioned Yugoslavs in Dublin and London. The Yugoslavs, both Communist and anti-Communist, had no information. A friend in London, who had been to Trinity College, Dublin, remembered someone saying: 'I'd like you to meet a very interesting chap called Anitch', but the meeting had never happened. In the end Branko Miljus, a former minister of the pre-war government in Belgrade, who now lives in Paris, got some news for me from a friend in Switzerland. If I seem to give too many names and details, it is so that his story can be checked and completed.

The first stage of the journey is fairly well known. Pavelitch and Artukovitch had escaped to Austria when the Croatian state collapsed..They seem to have been arrested by the British in Salzburg and, after 'a mysterious intervention', released and there was an interval of hiding in monasteries at Sankt Gilgen and Bad Ischl. The Yugoslavs were in hot pursuit, so Pavelitch fled to Rome, disguised as a Spanish priest called Gomez. Artukovitch stayed on till November 1946, when he met the learned Dr Draganovitch, Professor of Theology at Zagreb, who was touring the internment camps with a Vatican passport. He had secured the release of many hundreds of Croat priests who had fled with Pavelitch. Now he obtained for Artukovitch papers under the name Alowz Anitch and put some money for him in a Swiss bank. Two other priests, Fathers Manditch and Juretitch, also came to his aid. The former, the treasurer to the Franciscan order, controlled a printing press at the Italian camp of Fermo and assisted the Ustashe (Croatian nationalist) refugees with funds and propaganda. Juretitch had been sent on a mission to Fribourg by Archbishop Stepinac, so he and Manditch, both former students of Fribourg University, were able to secure a welcome there for Artukovitch. Archbishop Sharitch, Pavelitch's poet-champion, had got there ahead of him. Both Draganovitch and Juretitch had been appointed by Mgr Stepinac to the Commission of Five for the Conversion of the Orthodox in November 1941. These three were important people to have as sponsors. The ecclesiastics of Fribourg must have been impressed. They recommended Artukovitch to the police who got him a *permis de séjour.* There were other difficulties, which, according to report, Artukovitch smoothed out by the gift of a Persian carpet to an influential official.

But meanwhile the Federal Police had learnt that Anitch was the war criminal Artukovitch. They told him he had two weeks in which to leave Switzerland. Once more the Franciscans came to his aid. The prior of the Maison Marianum at Fribourg recommended him to the Irish Consulate at Berne. And so it happened that in July 1947 Artukovitch landed with his family on the Isle of Saints, sponsored by the disciples of that saint, who had prayed:

> Lord, make me an instrument of Thy peace!
> Where there is hatred let me sow love,
> Where there is sadness, joy!

I do not know where Artukovitch spent his Irish year, but one day, as a matter of history, and perhaps of religion, we shall have to know. If Artukovitch had to be carried half-way round the earth on the wings of Christian charity, simply because he favoured the Church, then Christianity is dying. And if now, for ecumenical or other reasons, we are supposed to ask no questions about him, then it is already dead.

On 15 July 1948 Artukovitch with an Irish identity card left Ireland for the USA where he settled as a book-keeper, near his wealthy brother in California, still under the name of Anitch. It was over two years before his true identity was discovered. The Serbian Orthodox were slow to move. Oppressed by the Communists at home, dispersed as refugees abroad, they still managed to publish the facts in books and papers in London, Chicago, Paris. In 1950 Branko Miljus, and two other prominent monarchist politicians in exile, sent a memorandum to the Fifth Assembly of the Unit-

— *The Artukovitch File* —

ed Nations urging it to implement its resolution of December 1946, which had branded genocide as a crime against international law. They asked that its member states should take into custody, till a Commission be appointed to try them, some 120 Croat nationals, who had taken refuge among them. On the long list appended, the names of Artukovitch, Archbishop Sharitch, Fathers Draganovitch and Juretitch and many Franciscans were mentioned, and some of the scarcely credible Franciscan story was related. It is stated that a Franciscan had been commandant of Jasenovac, the worst and biggest of the concentration camps for Serbs and Jews (he had personally taken part in murdering the prisoners and Draganovitch, with the rank of Lieut.-Colonel, had been the chaplain). The memorandum relates how the focal centre for the forced conversions and the massacres had been the Franciscan Monastery of Shiroki Brijeg in Herzegovina (Artukovitch had been educated there) and how in 1942 a young man who was a law student at the college and a member of the Catholic organization, The Crusaders, had won a prize in a competition for the slaughter of the Orthodox by cutting the throats of 1360 Serbs with a special knife. The prize had been a gold watch, a silver service, a roast suckling pig and some wine.

How can this be true? One recalls that great hero of Auschwitz, the Polish Franciscan Father Kolbe. But it *was* true and rumours of it had reached Rome. Rushinovitch, Pavelitch's representative at the Vatican, had reported to his Foreign Minister in Zagreb the remarks of Cardinal Tisserant, with whom he had an audience on 5 March 1942:

I know for sure that even the Franciscans of Bosnia-Herzegovina behaved atrociously. Father Shimitch, with a revolver in his hand, led an armed gang and destroyed Orthodox Churches. No civilized and cultured man, let alone a priest, can behave like that.

Tisserant had probably got some of his information from the Italian general of the Sassari division at Knin, who had reported that Shimitch had come to him as local representative of the Croatian Government and had told him that he had orders to kill all the Serbs. The general had had instructions not to interfere in local politics, so he could only protest. The killing, under Franciscan leadership, had begun. The following year the Superior of the Franciscan Monastery in Knin was decorated by Pavelitch for his military activities with the order of King Zvonimir III.

The Croat bishops themselves were aware of what was happening. The Bishop of Kotor, Dr Butorac, while agreeing that the moment was propitious for mass conversion, wrote to Mgr Stepinac (4 November 1941) that the wrong type of missionaries were being sent – 'priests in whose hands revolvers might better be placed than a crucifix'.

In parenthesis, I should say, how fascinating are

Rushinovitch's accounts of his audiences in Rome with Pius XII, with Cardinals Tardini, Maglione, Sigismondi and Spellman. Only Tisserant, and to a lesser extent Mgr Montini, the present Pope, appear to have fully grasped what was happening in Croatia. In Cardinal Ruffini the Ustashe had a firm supporter.

The memorandum made little impression on the United Nations, since it had no member-state behind it. It had accused Tito's Government, which *was* a member-state, of sheltering many Croat criminals and using them to break down the anti-Communist resistance of the Serbs. However, in 1952 Tito appealed to the USA for the extradition of Artukovitch. The California Courts to whom the case was referred argued that the extradition treaty of 1901 between USA and Serbia had never been renewed and that therefore Artukovitch could not be handed over to Yugoslavia. Six years later the Supreme Court rejected this view (by 7 to 1) and decreed that the case must be tried again in California. In the meantime Artukovitch had become a member of the Knights of Columbus and a much-respected figure who gave lectures to institutes and interviews on TV. When he was arrested again 50,000 Knights sent petitions on his behalf to Congress, and the West Pennsylvania Lodges of the Croatian Catholic Union forwarded a resolution that 'his only crime is his ceaseless fight against Communism' and that he was a champion of the rights and freedoms of all the peoples of the world.

That was the way his counsel, O'Connors and Reynolds, presented him, too, and Father Manditch, who had helped him in Switzerland, was once more by his side, in charge of another printing press and now Superior of the Franciscan Monastery in Drexel Boulevard, Chicago. His papers *Nasha Nada* and *Danica* (*Our Hope* and *Morning Star*) not only supported him but in their issues of 7 May 1958 urged their readers to send subscriptions for the Ustashe refugee fund to Artukovitch at his address in Surfside, California.

Another very useful ally was Cardinal Stepinac's Secretary, Father Lackovitch, who had sought asylum at Youngstown, Ohio. In Europe Stepinac had been almost beatified for his implacable hostility to Pavelitch and Artukovitch, but now *The Mirror News* of Los Angeles (24 January 1958) reported Lackovitch as saying that he had seen Artukovitch almost daily and that he had been 'the leading Catholic layman of Croatia and the lay spokesman of Cardinal Stepinac and had consulted him on the moral aspect of every action he took'. The murderers of the Old World had become the martyrs of the New.

The American public was so ill-informed that it was possible to get away with almost anything. Pattee prints a statement that 200,000 of the converts from Orthodoxy were returning 'with a right intention' to a Church, which 'for political reasons' they had been forced to abandon. In fact, of course, the Serbian Orthodox had been in schism for some three centuries before the Protestant Reformation. Cardinal Tisserant, who had a rare tolerance of disagreeable truths, denounced Rushinovitch vigorously when he tried out this argument on him:

I am well acquainted with the history of Christianity and to my knowledge Catholics of Roman rite never became Orthodox . . . The Germans helped you kill all the priests and you got rid of 350,000 Serbs, before you set up the Croatian Orthodox Church. What right have you to accuse others and keep on telling us that you are guardians of culture and the faith? In the war with the Turks the Serbs did just as much for Catholicism as you did and perhaps more. But it was the Croats, all the same, who got the title of *Antemurale Christianitatis.*

When I was in California, I went to see Father Mrvicin of the Serbian Orthodox Cathedral at West Garvey, near Los Angeles, and asked him why the Orthodox and the Jews of California had tolerated so many lies. He told me that at the time of the extradition trial he had circularized close on a thousand Serbs, who must have known well about Artukovitch, urging them to give evidence, but very few had replied. Life in the USA was hard for them as refugees, they did not want to affront a powerful community; McCarthyism was not yet dead and they were shy of associating themselves with an appeal that came from a Communist country. A naturalized American, who took the matter up, died violently and mysteriously.

— THE INVADER WORE SLIPPERS —

As for the Jews, though 30,000 with their 47 rabbis had been murdered in Croatia, Croatia was far away, and many who had escaped to the USA had owed their safety to holding their tongues. Even so, the Jewish War Veterans of California, *The Valley Jewish News* and some Gentile papers like *The Daily Signal* of California came out against Artukovitch. But most Americans felt for the unknown refugee and his five children the easy charity of indifference. Finally the Yugoslav Government did some profitable deals with the USA and became indifferent, too. It is now interested only in proving that Artukovitch was a helpless stooge of the Nazis and that therefore the Bonn Government should pay compensation to Yugoslavia for the damage that he and the Ustashe had done.

The other day I came across a *History of Croatia*, published by the New York Philosophical Library. The author, Mr Preveden, acknowledges various 'inspiring messages of commendation and encouragement'. One of them comes from 'Dr Andrija Artukovitch of Los Angeles'. He is quite a public figure. He may have changed his address but his telephone number used to be Plymouth 5-1147.

Now many people want him hanged but there would not be much point in it. He was an insignificant man, who got his chance because there had been a great breakdown in the machinery of Christianity and he was able to pose as its protector. Why did this breakdown occur? Can it be repaired and, if so, how?

— *The Artukovitch File* —

So long as we are obliged to pretend that the breakdown did not happen, we shall never find out.

Postscript 1971. There has since been an easing of tension between Communism and Christianity, most notably in Yugoslavia, where diplomatic relations with the Vatican have been resumed and there has been friendship between Catholic and Orthodox. For example, in a Christmas message, Bishop Pichler begged forgiveness of the Orthodox Church and their Serbian brothers for all the wrongs done to them and funds have been raised by Catholics to restore the destroyed Orthodox churches.

Some of the leading Orthodox are not wholly happy about all this. Is it spontaneous or Government inspired? Is it possible that Tito fears the deep-rooted and passionate nationalism of the Orthodox more than Catholic universalism, which can be manipulated by external arrangements? Under the amnesty to political offenders, many Ustashe have returned home, notably Father Draganovitch, one of the five 'regulators' of the Forced Conversions, who escorted Pavelitch and Artukovitch to safety. He is in a monastery near Sarajevo editing the Schematismus, a sort of ecclesiastical yearbook, whose publication has been suspended since 1939. Some of his returned colleagues are more active politically.

There is, of course, everything to be said for peace and conciliation, but the brotherly love that is brought about by diplomatic manoeuvres is often a little suspect.

II. IN SEARCH OF A PROFESSOR OF HISTORY

I could not get it out of my head that eighteen years before, Artukovitch had stayed for a year in Ireland. How had he come here? Who had sheltered him and where? In the spring of 1966 I was in Dublin for a week and I decided to find out. I was convinced that only some highly organized international body could have brought a wanted man so secretly and efficiently across Europe and, since the Franciscans had been so closely associated with the Ustashe in Croatia and had many international links I was confident that it was they who had brought him. I have never heard anything but good of Irish Franciscans but they were an institutionalized body and as such able and anxious to protect their members who get into trouble abroad.

There were a dozen Franciscan Houses in Ireland and I wrote to the Provincial in Merchant's Quay, Dublin, and also to four or five other houses, which, because of their remoteness, I thought were likely. Most of them answered with polite negative replies. The Provincial told me there had been a Croat Franciscan at their Galway house for some time but his name, Brother Ivanditch, was on the list of their Order and they had no doubt of his identity.

— *The Artukovitch File* —

It was not till Branko Miljus sent me his copy of *The Mirror News* of Los Angeles that I made any progress. Artukovitch had been interviewed by the reporter, Henry Frank, who for the photograph had arranged him at a piano, grouping his wife and five handsome children round him. The Rev. Robert Ross of the Blessed Sacrament Church was there too as a friend and advocate. He told Frank how, as Minister of the Interior, Artukovitch had helped the Jews and been a formidable foe to the Communists.

'Artukovitch listened gravely and said with quiet dignity, "I put my faith in God".'

Frank spoke of Artukovitch's 'strong, seamed face' and his 'modest well lived-in living-room'. He told how his daughter, Zorica, had won an essay competition in Orange County High School and his nine-year-old son, Radoslav, had been born in Ireland.

Here was a clue. The children had been exploited sentimentally to mask the truth, so they could be used to rediscover it. I went to the Customs House and after prolonged search I found Radoslav Anitch's birth certificate (A.164, No. 75). He was born on 1 June 1948 at the Prague House Nursing Home, 28 Terenure Road East; he was the son of Alois Anitch, Professor of History, of 6 Zion Road, Rathgar.

On the strength of this discovery, I sent a letter to all the Dublin dailies, explaining that I was writing an account of the Independent State of Croatia (1941–45) and that I wished information about the former

Minister of the Interior, Andrija Artukovitch (alias Alois Anitch), who had lived at 6 Zion Road, Rathgar, in 1947. Only *The Irish Times* printed my letter, turning him into a lady called Audrey.

In the meantime I visited the two houses, which were close to each other. No. 6 Zion Road is a two-storied house of red brick with an ivy-tangled sycambre and an overgrown privet hedge, but it had changed hands so often that it told me nothing about Artukovitch's Irish sponsors.

No. 28 Terenure Road, a tall building of red and white brick with much ornamental ironwork, has ceased for some years to be a nursing home. Nobody knew where the former owner had gone and it was not till I had paid two visits to the Guards Barracks at Terenure that one of them recalled where she now lived. It was not far off at 7 Greenmount Road and I went there immediately. The matron was a charming and intelligent woman and after eighteen years she remembered the Anitches perfectly. She had found them a pleasant and pathetic couple. He had spoken little English, Mrs Anitch had spoken fluently and, because of that, she had asked that he should have lunch with her in the Nursing Home. 'He is my baby,' Mrs Anitch had said, 'he wouldn't know how to get lunch without me.' They had two little girls who were at the Sacred Heart Convent, in Drumcondra Road, and now they wanted a boy. 'If it's a girl,' said Mrs Anitch, 'don't call him till the evening.' But when on the morning of 1 June

— *The Artukovitch File* —

Radoslav had been born, she was so delighted that she said her husband must be called at once. Anitch came and in his joy he had embraced the matron, much to her embarrassment. The Anitches had behaved nicely paying all their debts with money from America. After they had gone some months Mrs Anitch had written a grateful letter, which the matron showed me.

Only one person besides her husband had visited Mrs Anitch in the Nursing Home. He was a Franciscan who had been in Croatia, but the matron was not clear whether or not he was a foreigner. The Anitches had told her that the Communists had been particularly vindictive against the Franciscans.

My anticipations that the Franciscans had helped Artukovitch in Ireland had now been confirmed, so I went to see the Provincial at Merchants' Quay. This time he agreed with me that the friar at the Nursing Home must have been the Croat at the Galway House. His name, he said, was Ivanditch. He was a supporter of Pavelitch and had often gone from Galway to Dublin.

Yet a Croat friar could not have made all these arrangements without powerful Irish assistance. Where had it come from?

The process by which a great persecutor is turned into a martyr is surely an interesting one that needs the closest investigation. I had only four days left in Dublin, so I could not follow up all the clues, but I made some progress.

First I went to the Sacred Heart Convent, 40 Drumcondra Road, a big red building on the left hand side of the street. I was shown into a little waiting-room and was received by a charming and friendly nun. I told her I was trying to trace the family of two little girls called Zorica and Vishnya Anitch, who had been at the convent in 1947 when they were four and five years old. She went away to look them up in her register and I sat for a very long time contemplating the plate of wax fruit and the little figurine of St Anthony. Then the nun returned and told me that the two little girls (but they were called Katherina and Aurea Anitch) had been admitted on 9 August 1947. Their parents had lived at 7 Tower Avenue, Rathgar and had taken the children to USA on 15 July 1948. She did not recall them herself but suggested that I ring up an older nun, Sister Agnes, who would certainly remember them. She was at St Vincent's Convent, North William Street. I rang Sister Agnes, who remembered them all vividly. The little girls were sweet and she had found the two parents 'a lovely pair' and Dr Anitch was 'a marvellous musician'. She did not remember that anybody came to visit the children except their parents, but a Franciscan monk, a nephew of Dr Anitch's, who had escaped with them from Croatia, was with them and had helped them to find lodgings.

Next I visited 7 Tower Avenue and was directed to a previous tenant, who worked in an ironmongery in D'Olier Street. He said he did remember having a

— *The Artukovitch File* —

lodger with a name like Anitch. He added, 'He was black, you know.' I tried other houses in Tower Avenue. Everybody was helpful and interested but I got no further clues.

After this I returned to Mrs O'Donoghue in Greenmount Road and found she had been keenly interested in what I had told her and herself had been trying to find out who had been the landlord in 6 Zion Road when the Anitches had lived there. She said I should get in touch with Patrick Lawlor, 32 Hazelbrook Road, who had sold the house to some woman in 1947.

I wrote to him and the next day he rang me up. He said it was so long ago that he could not remember the woman's name, but the auctioneer might know. After that I made some dozen visits and twenty telephone calls. They would be boring to relate but I found them exhilarating, as each clue led to another clue. I telephoned the doctor who had delivered Radoslav and examined the parish registers in Terenure and Rathgar for christenings. I went to the Valuation Office and telephoned the Voters Register, the Irish Red Cross, the Aliens Office and the International Office of Refugees. I enquired at the City Hall about Corporation Rates. In the end I got onto the solicitor who had acted both for Mr Lawlor and for the woman to whom he had sold 6 Zion Road. His clerk made an unsuccessful search for her name and then suggested, 'Why not call on Thom's Directory?'

I went there the next day and the secretary took

down from a shelf the directories for 1947 and 1948 and found Patrick Lawlor's name in both. 'But that's impossible,' I protested. 'He sold the house to a woman in 1947.' 'Yes, but there might have been a delay in publishing after we collected the information.' She took down the directory for 1949. 'The woman's name was Kathleen Murphy,' she said. I was off like a shot to a telephone-box.

There were three Miss K. Murphys in the directory and five Mrs Kathleen Murphys and several K. Murphys, who might be either male or female. It was a lengthy business for some were out and I was asked to ring later and some were testy at being catechised by a stranger. The fifth answered very suspiciously. 'Who are you? Why do you want to know? Yes, I was at 6 Zion Road, but if you want to know more you must come down. I remember the Anitches and, if you're friends of theirs I'd be glad to see you. Do you know them?' I said I did not but that a friend of mine in Paris, M. Miljus, would like to get in touch with them.

So we drove down to 6 Barnhill Road, Dalkey, a fine broad street with handsome villas. My wife waited outside in the car writing letters, while Mrs Murphy, a friendly middle-aged woman talked to me in her drawing-room. A friend of hers was just leaving when I came in, an Ulsterwoman with a nice downright manner, whose husband had been a bank manager in Kilkenny. She remembered us straight off when I said my name. 'Yes, I know who you are. I read your letters and articles in *The Irish Times.* I remember you got into a row with the Nuncio, Dr O'Hara, and it was on the head of you he got the boot!' She and Peggy talked together while I was with Mrs Murphy, who I could see had a powerful affection for this foreign family who had lodged with her. In particular she admired 'Dr Anish', whom she connected with 'Czechoslavia'. This confusion is not very surprising. Artukovitch would not have mentioned Yugoslavia, which did not exist for him, and not much was known in Ireland of Croatia, though one of those who were kind to him in Dublin said he came from Craishe. In general he was befriended as a foreign refugee from Communism and hitherto I have found no trace of sinister international intrigue among those who gave him hospitality.

Mrs Murphy reproached herself repeatedly for not having kept in touch with the 'Anishes' in California. Several times they had written charming letters. What a delightful family they were! 'They made a wonderful impression all round,' she said. 'I'd like to show you some snaps I have of them.' Mrs Murphy took down a photograph album with a large bundle of snaps in the middle. She rummaged through them all the time we were talking but never found what she was looking for. I explained to her that some time after Dr Anitch had got to California he had been the subject of bitter controversy and I showed her the picture of the family in *The Mirror News.* 'Ah, how old he has got to look, poor man! And that big girl must be Katerina and that one Aurea. And goodness me that young chap must be Radoslav! How time flies!' When I told her what his enemies were saying she shook her head indignantly. 'People will say anything! I don't think he thought of politics at all. All he cared about was his family. He was a wonderful father and husband! He was a very good man you know. He was rather like President Kennedy. He wanted justice for everybody. And he loved the Church. They were daily communicants.' Then I asked her how she had met him in the first place and she said she thought it had been at some party. Maybe some priest had introduced them. She became a little vague on the whole in this pregnant conversation. I was being the sly one, she the candid one. I asked did she meet a Franciscan with him and she said, 'Oh, yes, there was one came to lunch a couple of times. But the Anishes lived very quietly. They hardly saw anyone. You see he was a very retiring scholarly man. He once or twice gave a lecture at UCD, but otherwise they just thought of the children.' I subsequently made enquiries about those lectures at UCD but with no success.

Then I told her what remorseless enemies he had and explained something of the collapse of Yugoslavia. I showed her *Artukovitch, the Himmler of Yugoslavia,* turning the pages rapidly so as to reach some not too emotive pictures of him in the days of his glory. There he was giving the Nazi salute to a German general and there again greeting Hitler's envoy at the head of his Security Police, and there with his wife at a cocktail

— *The Artukovitch File* —

party in the Hungarian Embassy. I skipped some horror pages, headed with heavy irony ANDRIJA ARTUKOVITCH'S HEROIC DEEDS and including a picture of a soldier scissoring off the head of a seated peasant with some shears. Except for their attribution, such photographs are probably genuine. As I have said, Artukovitch was probably a desk murderer only. Mrs Murphy must have caught a glimpse of the scissored head for she stiffened and started to fumble again in her album for her friendly snapshots.

'Everybody in Dublin seems to have liked him,' I said, 'but why did he come here with a false name?'

'Probably he was forced to. Lots of people are. He couldn't have been a Nazi, though he may have been forced to take that side. I'm a good judge of character. I've travelled in sixteen countries and know a good man when I see one.'

'But he signed all those laws against the Jews.' (I thought it would be too complicated to talk about the Orthodox; she might not know who they were.)

'Well, look what the Jews are doing to other people!' (I suppose she was thinking of the Arabs.)

Then we said good bye. As I left she repeated: 'They just lived for their children. They thought the world of them.'

The next place I had to visit was the Franciscan House in Galway from which Dr Anitch's nephew, Brother Ivanditch, paid visits to Dublin to see him.

When we reached Galway I went round to the Franciscan House, which is a few streets away from Eyre Square. Beside the big church I saw a small private door through which some travelling clerics with suitcases were being hospitably ushered. I waited till they had all been welcomed before I went in and, after a few moments, the Father Superior appeared. Though he was preoccupied with his visitors he received me kindly. Seeing my attaché case he thought I was a commercial traveller, but when I explained I had come as a historian interested to find out about a Croat friar called Ivanditch, who was in Galway in 1947, he said, 'I'm afraid I don't know the good man. I'm only here three years, but, if you come tomorrow, when we've a bit more time, I'll get Brother Bede onto you. He was here in 1947.'

The following day I went round to the Franciscan House at 30 and Brother Bede received me. Yes. He remembered Brother Ivanditch well and had looked him up in the 'Schematismus' of the Order. He was from the province of Bosnia, near Sarajevo. He was a very striking looking chap and must have been over six foot. He was born in 1913. 'He wasn't here but at our hostel, St Anthony's College along the Moycullen Road, so I didn't see much of him. But they say he spent all his time at the wireless listening to the news in German, French, Italian, Spanish; he was a very intelligent fellow, learnt English quickly. But he was broody, reserved and melancholy. All soul, you might say.'

— *The Artukovitch File* —

Brother Bede had spent the war years in Rome. In the Franciscan headquarters the Croats had been more prominent than any other Slav group. Apart from Father Manditch, the treasurer of the Order, there was Father Jelachitch, a great canon-lawyer, and Brother Balitch, an eminent palaeographer who had written about Duns Scotus. 'You've no idea what confusion there was in Rome at that time. As for us, we put all the Slavs in one basket, a terribly passionate lot. We couldn't unscramble them.'

'Who sent him here? Oh, I suppose it was the General of our Order in Rome. I think it was Schaaf at that time, but I could look that one up. It was a question of obedience, you know.'

I told him that the Ustashe ambassador to Rome, Rushinovitch, had been given audiences by many cardinals and had sent his impressions of them back to Zagreb. It was obvious that not only the Irish but all the clerics at Rome had been highly confused by what was happening in Croatia. Only Cardinal Tisserant, I said, had a clear idea. On the other hand Cardinal Ruffini was a vigorous supporter and protector of the Ustashe!

'Ruffini!' Brother Bede laughed. 'Yes, indeed. He was a Sicilian, a great nationalist! They are as excitable as the Slavs. We took everything they said with a pinch of salt.'

As for Ivanditch, he had stayed for about a year in Galway and then gone to Canada. But there was a ru-

— THE INVADER WORE SLIPPERS —

mour that he was in Valencia, Spain, now. He was still alive or he wouldn't be in the Schematismus.

Brother Bede did not think I would get much more information from St Anthony's College as they were always changing their staff there, but there was a Brother David who might remember him. 'Worth trying anyway. Cross the salmon-weir bridge and along the Moycullen Road till you come to a long grey building on the left.'

They were widening the road and the surface was terrible so it must have been very close to the Brothers' dinner-time when I got to St Anthony's. The most pleasant thing about the building was the fine stone wall, a new one, that surrounded it. Most of the Galway walls are still excellently built and of stone, as unlike as possible to the new walls of the midlands, which, maybe because of the rich stoneless soil, are built of concrete, which submits itself readily to many vulgar and modish fancies.

I waited in a very clean and polished parlour under a picture of Jesus meditating on the Mount of Olives, till Brother David came along. He and his colleague, Brother Edmond, remembered Ivanditch well, and Brother David showed me a photograph of himself and Brother Ivanditch and a Galway lady, Mrs O'Halloran. They were a handsome group. Ivanditch, whose religious name was Brother Louis (Croatian Luji), was dark, clean-shaven, spectacled. A pleasant serious person he looked in his long brown habit with its white cord.

— *The Artukovitch File* —

'But he was very hysterical,' Brother David said. 'He'd been sentenced to death by the Communists and he spent all his time listening to the ups and downs of Communism on the wireless. He was with us about a year, sent here by the General at Rome, waiting for instructions where to go. He was a professor of Dogmatic Theology. According to what he said, he was second-in-command to the Provincial at Zagreb. He had been given the seal of the Province of Croatia – he had it with him here – when the Provincial was imprisoned.'

I asked him if Artukovich (Anitch) had ever been to visit him. 'No, he had no visitors at all though once or twice he went to Dublin.'

'He brooded the whole time. He said the only hope for us was to have a third world war immediately. He thought us a very weak lot. There was a milk strike in Galway at the time and he could not understand why we did not settle it straight away by shooting the milkmen. And we should invade the six counties and settle that matter too *immediately*.'

'What amazed us about him,' Brother Edmond said, 'was the way he ate jam for breakfast . . . sometimes nearly a whole pot, and without any bread, just with a spoon. And though he got to know English very well, he used some very funny expressions. When we used to ask him if he would like another helping of anything, he would say, 'Thank you, no, I am fed up!' But he made a great friend in the town who could tell you more about him than I can, Joe O'Halloran of the Corrib Printing Works. He was working in O'Gorman's book shop in those days and he and Brother Louis used to see a lot of each other. Joe is the son of Mrs O'Halloran you saw in the snap shot.'

It was difficult to believe that the Galway Brothers belonged to the same order as the Ustashe Franciscans. What was nearest to Brother Edmond's heart was a scheme for building houses for the homeless by voluntary groups. He had been considering this idea, while he was with the Order in Louvain.

Joe O'Halloran was in a white coat working at the Corrib Printers when I called. He asked for a few moments to change and then he joined me at the Imperial Hotel and we had vodka and orange together. He had only been eighteen when Brother Ivanditch was in Galway, and he had been hugely impressed by this glamorous and passionate foreigner who had fled from his country under sentence of death, who had seen his Provincial sentenced to five years' penal servitude and his Primate, a world famous cardinal, condemned to sixteen years imprisonment by a Communist government. They had spent every Sunday together and Joe's parents had been equally captivated by this engaging person, who bore with him the seals of the Franciscan Order in Croatia and the responsibility to make its sorrows known to the world. It was his dream to establish a Croatian Seminary in Dublin. Ireland must know what Croatia had suffered and was still suffering in the name of Christ. She must know that the fate that had befallen Croatia awaited all Europe. They must be prepared.

Brother Luji counted on Joe O'Halloran's support in this sacred cause. But after a year the orders came from Rome for him to cross the Atlantic. He sailed from Liverpool to Montreal and Joe O'Halloran saw him off in Dublin. But though he had left Joe in charge of a sort of crusade, he had not replied at all regularly to his letters and slowly they had lost touch with each other. Joe learnt, though, that Brother Luji had been appointed chaplain to the Croat workers at Windsor, which is on the Canadian side of the Detroit river. They worked in the Ford factory at Dearborn and Brother Luji built for them the Chapel of St Joseph. Later on he had heard that he had been secularized and had left the Franciscan Order and it now occurred to Joe O'Halloran that this might have been because the French-Canadian Franciscans did not like Ivanditch's Croatian politics, which a few years later resulted in the murder of the Yugoslav consul in Stockholm and a curious entente with the Communists.

I asked about Artukovitch-Anitch and also about Count O'Brien, but Joe knew nothing of them. The only layman in Galway that Ivanditch saw was Mr O'Flynn, the County Manager, who invited him to tea, because his niece had once taught in Zagreb. Ivanditch had however told Joe that he had an uncle in Dublin who had been a Minister in the government of Croatia. Joe O'Halloran stressed that Ivanditch had totally failed to inflame the Franciscans in Galway and was very much disappointed in the Irish. He had been in Galway when the Republic was proclaimed in Eyre Square, and he was amazed that the Government had tolerated an opposition for so long. Why had not they just shot them?

In the past eighteen years Joe had changed. Ivanditch, were he to return, would no longer have the intoxicating effect which he had had on him as a very young man. In those days he had been puzzled that his elders should be so apathetic. For example, Father Felim O'Brien, a well-known Franciscan, had been lecturing in Galway and had treated very coolly Ivanditch's passionate appeals for a crusade. O'Brien was known all over Ireland for his dislike of 'liberalism'. Two or three years later, in 1950, he engaged Owen Sheehy-Skeffington in a long controversy in *The Irish Times*, later published as a pamphlet, on *The Liberal Ethic*. I had contributed to this controversy so I have kept some records of it. O'Brien had maintained that in Ireland we owe our freedom of expression more to the clerics than to the liberal doctrine of tolerance, and that in Europe the Catholic clergy are the chief champions of liberty.

We got back late from Galway and it was a day before I was able to look up Ivanditch in my books. I found only one reference to him. He was referred to on

— *The Artukovitch File* —

page 20 in the report of the Stepinac Trial, *Sudenje Lisaku, Stepincu, Salicu I Druzini*, in connection with the trial of the Provincial of the Franciscan Order, Father Modesto Martinchitch. The Provincial is said to have given Brother Luji (Ivanditch), an Ustashe, a large sum of money to enable him to escape abroad. Brother Luji was not one of the five friars who helped the Provincial bury the thirty-four trunks of Ustasha treasure under the confessional in the Franciscan Church in May 1945, and I find no record of any activities that in Communist eyes were criminal. I think that when he claimed to have been sentenced to death by the Communists, Ivanditch was trying to make himself more glamorous. He seems to have escaped early on with an ample travel allowance and the seals of the province. Whether or not Artukovitch was really his uncle, it may have been his task to escort him abroad in safety.

Since Brother Bede had mentioned Dr Balitch, the eminent palaeographer, at the Vatican, I looked him up in the vast book *Magnum Crimen* by Professor Victor Novak of Belgrade, not expecting to find anyone so scholarly and remote in this record of horror. But there he was on page 900. 'Brother Doctor Karlo Balitch, Professor at the Franciscan University at Rome.' His offence seems to have been slight but significant. When Marshal Kvaternik, the Commander of the Ustashe Forces, had arrived in Rome and visited the Institute of St Jerome in February 1942, Professor Balitch had been there to receive him, together with several other distinguished Croatian clerics and the whole staff of the Institute. Dr Balitch seems to have listened appreciatively while Dr Madjerec, the Rector, praised Kvatemik and the leader Pavelitch for their illustrious deeds in the cause of Christ.

The St Jerome Society was a very old and established Croat Institution with headquarters at Rome. Every year, even when Novak published his book in 1948, there were celebrations there in honour of Pavelitch's birthday, attended by Croat Jesuits, Dominicans, Capuchins, Benedictines. When Marshal Kvaternik addressed the Institute praising its work for the Ustashe there was loud and prolonged applause. This was in Rome, yet we have been told repeatedly that it was only under the strongest pressure that in Croatia itself the hierarchy lent their support to Pavelitch.

After the St Jerome Society had been suppressed in Croatia by Tito, Mgr Stepinac declared in his speech of defence: 'The St Jerome Society has ceased to exist. Its suppression is a grave offence against the whole people.' But surely it was rightly suppressed.

In an authoritarian community, when there is hypocrisy and connivance at the centre, the ripples from them spread outwards to the remote circumference: 'In vain do they worship me, teaching as their doctrines the precepts of men.'

In 1985 there is news of Dr Draganovitch, who helped Artukovitch to escape. I have been reading Tom

— *The Artukovitch File* —

Bower's story of Barbie, 'the Butcher of Lyons' who eluded French justice after the war in 1951 by the 'Rat Line', an escape-route which the Americans set up for people who were valuable to the CIA. They were equipped with fake passports and identity cards, but a contact was needed in Genoa, the port of embarkation, to supply the Rats with immigration papers for South America. Draganovitch, who had helped so many Ustashe escape to the Argentine, was obviously the man for the job. His fees for the Rat Line, according to Tom Bower, were $1,000 for adults, half-price for children and $1,400 for VIP treatment.

Surprisingly, though his services to the escaping Ustashe were well-known and though he had been on the infamous Committee of Five for the conversion of the Orthodox, he was permitted legally to return to Yugoslavia.

Is it possible that just as Barbie had useful information to give the Americans about the Communists, so Draganovitch had useful information to give the Communists about the Americans?

Artukovitch himself is still in California and, as I have related, sometime in the sixties the Yugoslav Government tired of asking for his extradition. Among other reasons, maybe, they thought that a sensational state trial in Zagreb might revive animosities between Serb and Croat.

However, in July 1981, the Board of Immigration Appeals in the USA, in view of a 1979 ruling of Congress, ordered that Artukovitch be deported. This was followed by further legal proceedings, appeals, counter-appeals, hearings and re-hearings.

In spring 1984 a civil suit against Artukovitch was filed in Los Angeles by relatives of twelve Yugoslav Jews murdered 'in the death camps'. An *Irish Times* report (2 April 1984) said, 'US officials familiar with the case always expressed puzzlement at how Artukovitch obtained sanctuary in Ireland and then received a visa to visit the US where his brother, a contractor/lived.' How much of the puzzle have I solved?

The US Justice Department acted on a legal reform excluding 'Nazi collaborators' from seeking refuge and on 14 November 1984 'three carloads of federal marshals, guns drawn', burst into Artukovitch's house at Seal Beach and took him into custody (*The Sunday Times,* 12 January 1985). He is now eighty-five and, according to his Dublin-born son Radoslav, he has Parkinson's Disease, a congestive heart condition, and is also blind and suffering from delusional paranoia. It is uncertain whether he will be competent to take part in an extradiction hearing and its sequel, deportation to Yugoslavia and a show-trial at Zagreb.

– The Kagran Gruppe –
[1988]

I believe one of the happiest times of my life was when I was working for the Austrian Jews in Vienna in 1938–9. It is strange to be happy when others are miserable, but all the people at the Freundeszentrum in the Singerstrasse were cheerful too. The reason surely is that we have always known of the immense unhappiness that all humanity has to suffer. We read of it in the newspapers and hear it on the radio but can do nothing about it.

Most people tied to a single job or profession die without exercising more than a tenth of their capacities. In the Singerstrasse for many months all my faculties were engaged and I exercised an intimate control over the lives of a great many people, and I believe I helped them.

Hitler brought into the world misery such as no man had previously conceived possible. It had to be combated. The British were slow to observe this. The Irish never did. As late as 1936 Lloyd George went to Germany and told Hitler he was the greatest German of his age. London's society hostesses flocked round Ribbentrop and received invitations to the Olympic Games which, thanks to Goebbels, were a huge success. Predictably, the poor silly Duke and Duchess of Windsor visited the Führer.

The mood in Ireland was one of ignorant indifference. It was expressed in the Dàil in 1943 by a very pious Catholic, Oliver Flanagan. 'There is one thing', he said 'that the Germans did and that was to rout the Jews out of their country.' He added that we should rout them out of Ireland: 'They crucified our Saviour 1900 years ago and they have been crucifying us every day of the week.' No one contradicted him.

But I was as Irish as Oliver Flanagan and I was determined that Jewish refugees should come to Ireland. At the time of the Anschluss the Quakers were settled in the Freundeszentrum in Vienna and through Friends' House in London I got permission to join them. The Freundeszentrum was a former nobleman's palace in the Singerstrasse and when I got there, together with a charming and energetic young Quaker called Mary Campbell, I was put in charge of the Kagran Gruppe, a group of Viennese Jews who had banded together for collective emigration.

My first few weeks at the Freundeszentrum were spent at a desk filling in hundreds of 'bogen', or emigration forms, for the crowds of applicants who turned up. After the usual questions about age, religion, profession, married or single, the women were asked, 'Can you cook, wash, scrub, knit?' The men had a corresponding questionnaire. Almost all the questions were answered in the affirmative. At the bottom one added

— *The Kagran Gruppe* —

one's comment. I do not know what happened to the stacks and stacks of bogen. Probably they were forwarded to the Friends' House in Euston Road and carefully filed. What would we have done if some instinct had told us of Auschwitz? Why was I the only non-Quaker there?

I think now it was obtuse of us not to have anticipated Auschwitz. I had walked along the Prater Strasse to the Prater, the great Viennese Park where bands played and stalls sold ice cream and coffee. The street must have had a great many Jewish shopkeepers in it, because all the way down there were broken windows in front of looted shops with VERHOLUNG NACH DACHAU ('Gone for a rest-cure to Dachau') scrawled over the surviving panes, and the air was full of the mindless hatred which war, that fosters all our basest passions, would inevitably make murderous.

I speak German and French so I was shortly sent to the Conference on the problem of the German Jews at Evian, by the Lake of Geneva. The League of Nations had at last got to work and it was attended by representatives of all the countries in Europe and America. Vague gestures of goodwill were made. I talked to the two delegates from Ireland, or rather from the Irish Embassies in Paris and Berne. One remarked, 'Didn't we suffer like this in the Penal Days and nobody came to our help.'

When I got back I visited all the embassies to get visas for the emigrating Jews. There was a kindly official at the Mexican embassy who would sign an entry visa for anyone who asked. Even though it might fail to get them into Mexico it would get them out of Austria. So many applicants arrived that he had to get his wife and family in to help him.

One day I visited the Peruvian embassy. It was a splendid building with a large map of Peru painted on the staircase. I entered a spacious room with well-filled bookcases and handsome furniture. At the far end was a small figure seated at a large desk. I assumed he was the Peruvian ambassador, though in fact it was probably the consul. After the Anschluss the ambassadors had all been transferred to Stuttgart or Berlin. I appealed to him to persuade his government to admit Viennese Jews. He looked at me doubtfully and then said: 'I was wondering if you could help me. You see, I too am a Jew and want to get out as soon as possible. I've just written a letter to Churchill. Do you think that a good idea?' 'It would be much better to write to Emma Cadbury,' I replied. He bowed but looked too proud to be interested.

At this time the Bolivian consulate was one of the most thronged in Vienna. The report had got round that land was being given to agriculturalists on favourable terms, and that engineers and craftsmen were required. Of the many that applied only a very few were accepted. In the autumn a group of about 200 Jews were urged to prepare immediately for the journey. While the relief organizations hurriedly helped with

— *The Kagran Gruppe* —

the official formalities, they themselves sold their possessions with desperate haste for whatever they could get for them. They kept only the barest necessities for the journey and such goods as they could carry in their trunks to their new home A few days before the boat was due to sail they were informed that there had been a misunderstanding between the Gestapo and the Bolivian Consulate. No visas would be given for Bolivia and the expedition could not set off. The 200 settlers, now without homes or property, had to wander round the streets looking for hospitality from their friends.

At Eichmann's trial in Jerusalem in 1961 it emerged that he personally was responsible for providing the field in which the Kagran Gruppe was trained. When he was in Vienna emissaries from Palestine had approached him for help in the illegal immigration of Jews into British-ruled Palestine. 'He was polite,' they said, 'and even provided a farm and facilities for setting up vocational training camps for prospective immigrants. On one occasion he expelled a group of nuns from a convent to provide a training camp for young Jews.'

Eichmann, like other Nazis in the early days, was sympathetic to Zionism and this lasted till 7 November 1938 when Ernst von Rath, the Third Secretary of the German embassy in Paris, ironically an anti-Nazi, was murdered by a 17-year-old Jewish youth Herschel Grynzpan, whose family had been deported to Poland. This led to Kristallnacht in November 1938, when all the synagogues in Berlin went up in flames, 7,500

Jewish shop-windows were smashed and 20,000 Jews were taken off to concentration camps. This increased the tension in Vienna and ever more people joined the Kagran Gruppe.

I found a letter of that time describing the desperate atmosphere to my wife:

There was a meeting yesterday of the leading Jews. I was very much moved by their courage and seriousness and idealism and innocence, as it seemed to me. They spent about twenty minutes deciding whether they should take their mahogany sideboards and bamboo hat-racks by ship or not and describing them. They have to go first to Sweden (that is to say if anything comes of the scheme at all and they can raise £14,000) and then after they've had their 'umschulung' training in agriculture there, they go off to somewhere like Paraguay, or, if they are lucky to Colombia, where there is some sort of community settlement already. I said that even shipping furniture from Belgrade to Dubrovnik, as we had done, was far dearer than selling it and then buying new stuff. They looked shocked and I realized I had said something hurtful and callous about their homes, and that to many its furniture was an intimate part of their lives. They had grown up with it and it was full of memories. This was 'Papa's chair and this was Mutti's' and the more stuck in their ways and the more entrenched they are, the more terribly touching it is. However, I'm glad they did decide to bring only the most cherished pieces. This afternoon when I was alone the Controller of Foreign Currency in the biggest bank but one – quite a swell with an almost complete set of gold teeth – pleaded to be allowed to join the camp with his wife and go out with them.

— *The Kagran Gruppe* —

He produced an armful of testimonials, but how could he be any use there?

But the real time for seeing people is between nine and one thirty. I see about ten and by the time one has reached the tenth one is utterly drained of sympathy and ideas and resourcefulness. I just gaze at them and put a new nib in the pen and rearrange the papers on the desk. In some cases it's just a matter of advice, how to find the address of a relation in Cairo or Cincinnati or something like that. There is a tremendous drive on now to Aryanize all the gemeindehauser (blocks of flats) and private houses along main streets where flags have to be hung on important occasions. As a result four people who came to me yesterday have had a notice to quit by August 1st and nowhere to go. They might get taken in as tenants by a Jewish landlord, but what are they to do with their furniture? Aryans who take Jewish lodgers also are liable to lose their flats. There was one old gentleman yesterday with an ear-trumpet in a state of mind about his flat. It belonged to his wife's daughter who was illegitimate and consequently happened to be Aryan, but he was terrified of disgracing her by living with her and was going to move out. Another couple had married Aryanized daughters who were very anxious to suport them, but for the same reason they were frightened of embroiling them and wanted to emigrate. There was an old officer with a testimonial from his General about his bravery at the battle of Przemysl.

It's such a relief when one comes on a really nasty one, as one does, e.g. a Feinkost Erzeuger (maker of delicatessen), with a horrible Aryan wife who wanted to know if the Friends' House in Philadelphia would get her an affidavit if she became a Quaker. Then there was a young police-officer, very well-educated, and a dark scared fanatical writer on a fashion paper, dozens and dozens of Beamter, Buchalter, Mechaniker, Techniker and chauffeurs and garage proprietors. There was one young Jew who had become a Nazi and hoped to become an honorary Aryan but wasn't accepted. And yesterday at the end two women and a little girl turned up. I was so fuddled by that time I can't remember what they wanted but they suddenly quite spontaneously and untheatrically all three began to snivel.

A plump dark-haired woman, a Nazi named Baronin Rikki von Appell, was always straying into the Friends' Centre. I think her job was to keep us under observation and she was particularly concerned about me as I was not a Quaker. She knew about Quakers and remembered the good work they had done in Vienna in 1920; the Viennese were starving so the Quakers among other projects imported 1,500 cows from Holland, to provide milk.

But what was I up to, a non-Quaker? She was puzzled and asked me to join her and a friend on a boating-trip on the Danube. We started from Klosterneuburg and I was enchanted with the unspoilt beauty, the water lilies and scarlet willows growing beside the river bank so close to a great city. Her friend was a thin fair-haired woman with a slight limp. She told me she had been engaged to be married, but because of her limp the Nazis, for genetic reasons, refused to allow it. She did not seem particularly resentful. I satisfied Rikki's curiosity by telling her that, like the Quakers, I

— *The Kagran Gruppe* —

had come out to help the Jews. She said the Jews were parasites who had speculated on the dwindling value of the Austrian crown after 1918. I did not accept this but was too ignorant to comment.

If I'd been a Quaker I would have said that the Quakers would help anyone who was suffering unjustly. The Quakers helped the Social Democrats when in 1934 Chancellor Dollfuss, a so-called Christian Socialist or Fascist, had crushed them. In Emma Cadbury's brilliant account of this period, *A Three-Day War and Its Aftermath,* she wrote that this civil conflict in Austria was one of the main causes of the Second World War. The Nazi takeover of Austria without opposition from England or France had made Czechoslovakia, now surrounded on three sides, an easy victim which the great powers would hesitate to defend.

Had it not been for the Three Days' War Austria should have been well able to defend itself against the Nazis. Democracy had been growing there as in Germany before the collapse of the two empires in 1918, and in Austria the Social Democrats (socialists) then became the dominant power in Vienna. Emma Cadbury describes all that they did for the workers' libraries, adult education, hospitals, clinics, and above all housing. Before the war 73 per cent of the people had been living in two rooms or less. In 1922, 60,000 houses were built with space for trees and grass and flowers. It was a superb achievement.

'Thus,' writes Emma Cadbury, 'life was made easier

for the proletariat and Communism found no foothold in Vienna.' But the Social Democrats had their enemies. Chief among them were the Christian Socialists, who were strongly influenced by the Catholic Church. They were extremely hostile to Hitler but regarded the Social Democrats as enemies of the Church who were impoverishing the middle and upper classes by overtaxation. The Social Democrats were ready to cooperate in fighting Hitler but the Christian Socialists could not wait. On 12 February 1934, with the approval of Chancellor Dollfuss, the Austrian army with the help of the Heimwehr, the army of the Christian Socialists, and the police made an assault on the Social Democrats. They and their army, the Schutzbund, were no match for the forces allied against them. Nearly 2,000 were killed and some 5,000 wounded. Many were executed and imprisoned. The Quakers were quickly on the scene distributing food with funds that came through the International Federation of Trade Unions.

The Austrian Nazis must have taken heart when they saw this great split in the ranks of their opponents. On 25 July 1934, a group of them broke into the Chancellery and shot Dollfuss. It was thought that this might lead to an immediate-Nazi takeover. But Schuschnigg managed to forestall this move and thirteen of the assassins were hanged.

Schuschnigg was summoned to Berchtesgarten and was bullied into signing a capitulation; as he had

— *The Kagran Gruppe* —

hoped, President Miklas refused to endorse it. Then he decided to hold a plebiscite, appealing for Social-Democratic support, promising to free their members from prison. March 14th, 1938, was to be the Great Day.

The vote would certainly have gone against the Nazis, so on 12 March, Hitler strutted into Austria. He crossed the frontier at Braunau and received a riotous welcome near Linz, his birthplace. Cardinal Innitzer ordered all the church bells in Austria to be rung. Schuschnigg was thrown into prison in the Gestapo headquarters and later was transferred to Dachau.

It was some months after this that I came to Vienna.

Typical of many is the story of the first Austrians I brought to Ireland. Erwin Strunz, an 'Aryan' with a Jewish wife and two small children, had been a trade union secretary with promise of a career in parliament in the Social Democratic Party till Dollfuss took over the government and routed the socialists. The Strunzes had no friends abroad and with a small son and a new-born baby they could not cross on foot over the mountains into Switzerland.

Erwin was advised by his Jewish friend Dr Schonfeld, President of the Austrian Atheists Association, to visit the Quaker Centre in Vienna. He had called on many Labour leaders and ecclesiastics. None of them could help. Then he remembered the work the

Quakers had done in starving Vienna in 1920. With a letter from Dr Schonfeld he visited Emma Cadbury at the Freundeszentrum. It was there I first met them at my desk and filled in their two bogen. Erwin told me he was an atheist and Lisl, who had big black eyes and a lively but firm expression, said to me, 'I will be a Mohammedan if it will help my children.' I entered them both as 'konfessionslos' (without Church), which in fact was the creed of very many Viennese Jews.

Emma Cadbury gave permission for 200 Kagraners to meet in the Quaker Centre and discuss their plans. They begged her to help them emigrate and form an agricultural co-operative overseas. Erwin and Lisl went early every morning with little Peter and all the others on the long tram journey to Kagran, a suburb on the left bank of the Danube. The group worked under the supervision of armed guards from the Gestapo who relished watching middle-aged Jews, many of them once rich sedentary businessmen, cutting trees, digging irrigation trenches, making a road; men who had never before held a shovel in their hands. They worked all the summer, while Emma Cadbury, Mary Campbell and I tried desperately to get entry permits for them to Peru, Bolivia, Rhodesia, Colombia, Canada. As I had already realized at Evian, nobody wanted them.

Erwin and his wife were in great danger. They slept every night in fear of the heavy knock at 5 a.m., the hour usually chosen by the Gestapo for the departure to Dachau. The Viennese Nazi Party thought

— *The Kagran Gruppe* —

there might be leader material in Erwin so the Party solicitor offered to arrange a divorce. He would be housed, temporarily, in the factory to avoid painful meetings with his ex-wife and children, and a blue-eyed Nazi woman had agreed to marry him. He was told he was lucky as she had a house of her own and some money. He would ultimately be transferred to the synthetic petrol factory at Dusseldorf and allotted a car, a monoplane and a villa. He could attend the university and later be drafted to the Party Leader School in Nuremberg. It was a dazzling offer so when he did not reply the Party grew suspicious. He hurriedly took sick-leave and simulated a nervous breakdown while still digging at Kagran. The Gruppe had seemed to be a way out of his difficulties, but now the future looked very menacing.

On 16 September 1938 he was rung up after midnight: 'Erwin. You have 48 hours to get out. Your arrest and deportation to Dachau has been decided.' He recognized the voice; it was a friend who had joined the Nazi Party but worked on behalf of the underground. (There were many such.) Erwin was thunderstruck, for though he had anticipated trouble he had not expected it so soon. He came to me next day in the Singerstrasse so hopeless and dispirited he could hardly speak. I finally found out what had happened and explained the situation to Emma Cadbury. After a good deal of telephoning, somehow she obtained entry permits for England which arrived within two hours.

— THE INVADER WORE SLIPPERS —

The Kagran Gruppe had set aside funds for the fares of emigrants which Hans Koch had entrusted to the treasurer, Viktor Strasser, and they were kept in a moneybox with two keys of which Koch had one, but when he went to get the fare for the Strunz journey he found the box empty. Strasser had stolen it all. We were forced to apply, as often before, to the Gildemeester Fund. (Gildemeester was a Dutch philanthropist to whose outstanding generosity in these terrible times I have seldom seen any reference.) The Strunzes got off on the train to Ostend and I telephoned to Peggy, my wife, to meet them at Charing Cross. After they arrived in London, owing to the strain of recent weeks, Erwin had a genuine breakdown and Peggy took them all back to her mother's home at Annaghmakerrig in Co. Monaghan.

After my own departure from Vienna I went on trying to get accommodation for the Kagran Group in Ireland and England, but Mary Campbell, who had been in charge of it with me in Vienna, was drafted by the Quakers to other work and replaced by a woman who knew nothing of Vienna or Kagran and did not speak German, so the heart went out of the idea of group emigration. She simply selected those most easy to place. In this way she was able to dispose of Hecht, the Kagran bee-keeper, Kalan, one of the very few agriculturalists, and Weinberg, our butcher and his wife: she was delighted with herself for this achievement, particularly when she had her picture in the *Daily Mirror.*

— *The Kagran Gruppe* —

We were left with a goldsmith, seven academics, a hairdresser, an umbrella maker, and many clerks, teachers and shopkeepers. It soon emerged that simply shelter and support in a friendly ambience was all that could be organized. This we achieved through the generosity of various private people in Ireland such as Arland Ussher in Cappagh, Co. Waterford, and Sir John Keane at Ardmore. I went to Bunnaton, a youth hostel in Donegal that was empty in the winter months. The parish priest, Fr O'Doherty, wanted to build a road from Bunnaton to Port Salon and hoped the refugees would help him. We also found places in England for three groups of Kagranners. Inevitably in Ireland the sectarian question arose and, I believe, our Irish Refugee Committee was unwittingly to blame for this. Members of committees seem always to be chosen to represent different interests whereas they should only have one interest, in this case the defence of the persecuted.

The long peace was about to end and the fate of the Jews had not precipitated that 'saeva indignatio' in the rest of Europe that would have given encouragement to the many hundreds of thousands of non-Jewish Germans who hated Hitler and, in 1944, welcomed the rising against him. Thousands must have died fighting for a Fatherland that had betrayed them.

Lately I came across a newspaper report of 10 December 1938 which I had cut out at this time. It tells of a great meeting in the Mansion House, London, on behalf of the Jews. The Archbishop of Canterbury spoke of 'the systematic persecution without parallel even in the Middle Ages', and the 'incredible mental and moral torture' to which the Jews were being subjected. Cardinal Pacelli sent the following telegram:

> The Holy Father's thoughts and feelings will be correctly interpreted by declaring he looks with humane and Christian approval on every effort to show charity and give effective assistance to all those who are innocent victims in these sad times of distress.

The tone of these two communications is very different. The Archbishop is explicit, the Cardinal is vague and general, but I do not think one can argue from this that the Englishman's heart was the warmer. It is the difference between the leader of a more or less homogeneous body and the head of a worldwide and heterogeneous community of believers. The Pope had followers in every land, all the Archbishop's were in one. Our disappointment in Pius XII springs from the delusive hopes that have been placed in universalism, in ecumenism. Now we know that if Christendom were ever to speak with one official voice, it would be a mouse's squeak. There would be so many conflicting sympathies to reconcile that in the end silence might seem best.

Catholics claim the Pope was impotent and I believe that was so. For example it was said that the Pope

— *The Kagran Gruppe* —

saved 400,000 Jews in Hungary. But these Jews owed their lives principally to the fact that Roosevelt had followed up an ultimatum about the deportations with a tremendous bombardment of Budapest on 2 July 1944.

As it happens, we were all wrong about the 400,000. It emerged at the Eichmann trial that he had defied all the neutral nations, Roosevelt and the Pope, and deported 1,500 Hungarian Jews in mid-July, and in October the shortage of labour in Germany was so great that they asked for a further 100,000. Since trains were no longer running, they were obliged to walk. Of Hungarian Jews, some 100,000 survived.

Some are surprised that people are not more impressed by the compliments paid to the Vatican by the Jewish leaders and the fact that the Rabbi of Rome even gave up his Jewish faith. But are the few who are dragged ashore entitled to give thanks on behalf of the millions who drowned? And is it not easy to undervalue the formidable social power of the community? The Jews were penniless refugees in foreign lands. Would many countries (Ireland for example) have accepted them readily if they had publicly claimed that the Pope or the Church had failed them in their hour of need? The Austrians who came to Ireland never even blamed Cardinal Innitzer, the Austrian Primate, who ordered all the church-bells in Austria to be rung when Hitler entered Austria to forestall the plebiscite. In reply to Cardinal Pacelli's cautious telegram, they themselves sent a very grateful one from Ireland to Rome. The Jews have reason to be apprehensive, even when a non-Jew like Hochhuth criticizes the Pope on their behalf. When *The Representative* was played in Paris, demonstrators leapt into the auditorium crying 'A bas les Juifs!'

It is clear that in times of stress parliaments and Churches are peculiarly subject to mass-pressure and one cannot expect too much from them. Nobody, whatever his faith, who had read the fulsome greeting from the leaders of the Evangelical Church in Austria to Hitler, 'the Tool in the hands of the Almighty' and 'the Fulfiller of the Divine Will for the Salvation of our People', could be confident that his own Church would have shown greater courage or foresight.

In the twentieth, as in the first century, we find the burden of Christianity borne by solitary and often anonymous individuals.

nh Notting Hill Editions

Notting Hill Editions is devoted to the best in essay writing. Our authors, living and dead, cover a broad range of non-fiction, but all display the virtues of brevity, soul and wit.

Our books are only part of our offering. Our commitment to reinvigorating the essay as a literary form extends to our website, where our Essay Journal is regularly updated with newly commissioned short essays as well as news and opinions on essay writing. The website also hosts a wonderful Essay Library, a home for the world's most important and enjoyable essays, including the facility to search, save your favourites and add your comments and suggestions.

To discover more, please visit
www.nottinghilleditions.com